Foreward

In Minneapolis, as in many cities, we often pass by people holding signs at intersections or standing quietly outside convenience stores. We look away. We roll up windows. We tell ourselves stories to explain their presence, stories that protect our comfort, but too often rob them of dignity.

This book asks us to stop and look again.

Will You See Me? is not just a question, it's a plea. A call to move beyond quick judgments, beyond surface impressions, and beyond the learned indifference that numbs us to the pain and resilience of our unhoused neighbors.

The individuals in these pages live without what many of us take for granted: safety, stability and a place to call home. But what they do not lack is humanity. Many live with integrity; most of us cannot imagine choosing honesty over easy escapes, generosity in the midst of scarcity, and hope even when the world keeps turning its back.

This book exists:
- To humanize those who are often overlooked by society.
- To inform our collective compassion, so it is not rooted in pity but in respect.
- To soften our cynicism toward those who may behave in ways we don't understand — because survival sometimes looks messy from the outside.

These stories will not solve homelessness. But they might just shift something in you. And maybe that's where change begins — not with sweeping solutions, but with a willingness to see.

So the next time you're at a red light and someone holds a sign asking for help, you may still choose not to give. But you'll know there is more to their story. And maybe, just maybe you'll meet their eyes.

Because they are asking: Will you see me?

— Pastor Chris Bellanger Sr.
Founder/Executive Director Unite Twin Cities

*I am not lost,
but I am forgotten.*

*I am full of dreams,
but I cannot reach them.*

*I am not whole,
but I am here.*

*I am a human,
but you are not me.*

*I am not hidden,
but will you see me?*

May this collection of personal stories open our eyes and hearts to intentionality and to notice those who may cross our paths each day.

We value your support and would love to hear from you and stay connected. To learn more about the Will You See Me? (WYSM) movement, please go to the following link to invite us to share with your group and register for newsletters, books, blogs, and training materials.

willyouseeme.com

"Do all the good you can, By all the means you can, In all the ways you can, In all the places you can, At all the times you can, To all the people you can, As long as ever you can." — J. Wesley

Published in 2025 by Books By The Bundle
Booksbythebundle.com
Minneapolis, MN

Copyright Shawn Morrison and Shawn Nielsen, 2025
All Rights Reserved

No part of this book may be reproduced, scanned, or distributed in any printed or electronic form without written permission from the authors.

ISBN: 979-8-218-71978-4

Library of Congress Control Number: 2025913220

———

Cover and Interior Design: Jim Lingenfelter,
Ignition Creative Solutions, ignitioncreativesolutions.com
Photography: Nielsen Studios, nielsen-studios.com
Editing: Scott Whitman, content creator and communications professional
Editing: Jamie Morrison, Books By The Bundle, booksbythebundle.com
Content support: Elisabeth Korth, narrativenuance.com

Introduction

For more than 30 years I've had the privilege to work closely with those who struggle to survive. I've met the urban poor, those experiencing homelessness, individuals with mental health concerns, and persons struggling with addiction and substance abuse. On occasion, these distraught souls have invited me to sit down with them, simply needing someone to listen with a sympathetic heart. They each recounted a unique personal journey fraught with heart-wrenching stories of abuse, neglect, shame, and the absence of personal stability. These sacred conversations have allowed me to witness firsthand how judgment-free listening can be a healing balm to a soul, particularly one that is starving for human validation. As we envisioned this project, I have found that these previous encounters provide a valued guiding influence.

With the ongoing economic challenges in our broader society, we have seen a marked increase in curbside begging. I suspect many of us are asking, "Why don't those who panhandle simply get a job?" Or, perhaps we wonder, "Are they scamming?" Or, "If we give money, will it be used for illicit purposes?" We may even find ourselves avoiding eye contact with people who fly signs to avoid the inner turmoil that often accompanies these unspoken solicitations.

This stirred me to consider my role, asking myself, "How can I foster a humane approach towards people who are typically seen as merely a public nuisance?"

As I contemplated what to do, I began to sense a compelling desire to personally connect with these fellow human beings. Rather than sitting back and holding my assumptions from afar, I wanted to learn firsthand, on the streets, some of the challenges and unique perspectives held by those who panhandle to survive. I wondered what I might do and what it might look like to provide these mostly unheard ones with an opportunity to share their stories.*

Getting started was not as easy as I had initially expected. Finding a willing and qualified professional photographer to partner with me for this meaningful project was challenging. That is, until I met Mr. Shawn Nielsen, owner of Nielsen Studios. He attentively listened to my strong interest in understanding and connecting with these overlooked souls who have endured a lifetime of difficult circumstances, often aggravated by their own poor choices. With an open heart, Shawn kindly agreed to partner with me for this significant project.

I'm forever grateful for our friendship and the many ways Shawn has sacrificially invested himself as a co-collaborator in this endeavor. Shawn's superior gift of photography has successfully captured each person in a way that is unlike any other I've seen. With well-honed instincts and a faithful desire to represent each individual with dignity, Shawn has successfully captured the essence of our participants. Perhaps even more impressive is his gift of self-effacing humility and the genuine care Shawn brings for those so often treated as the "have-nots" of our society, the present-day "untouchables." — Reverend Shawn Morrison

---

In his own heartfelt manner, Shawn Nielsen shares the following:

For many years, I passed by those who panhandled to survive. I never really saw them. I never made real eye contact with them. Then Shawn Morrison asked me to create photographic images for this project.

To be honest, we wrestled with the title 'Will You See Me.' Our first working title was 'Can You See Me'. Those four words didn't seem quite right, though. It left room for the viewer to look past the person. We eventually settled on "Will You See Me," a title asking the viewer to engage, to really take action, and really see our fellow humans.

We thought maybe, just maybe, this project would help others to look past the sign, stop being cynical about why they might really be there, and truly see this fellow human being. Ultimately, to see the heart of another person who simply needs someone, anyone, including you and me, to 'see' them.

Words can never truly explain how deeply this project has impacted me. Working alongside Shawn Morrison, I was given the chance to see what compassion in action looks like. This man has a huge heart for his fellow human beings and meets them where they are. He doesn't just talk about it. He really does it. Shawn Morrison is a man focused on living with an intentional kindness that changes our world. It changed me.

When I first said "yes" to the project, I didn't know it would have such a profound effect on me. I just knew it was a project that I couldn't say "no" to. I thought my reasons for saying yes were more about the artistic aspects (I've done a lot of 'people photography' over the last two decades). I quickly learned, however, that my involvement was more about opening my eyes and heart to care for people and maybe, alongside the words of Shawn Morrison, help share the true depth of their stories.

My hope is that you, too, will allow these stories to impact you as you read them. It's hard to fully digest what has brought each person to this place where they are so desperately asking for help. Take your time. Maybe read just one story and let it sit with you for a while. I fear that if you read them all in one sitting, it might be too overwhelming to take in, and you may miss the depth of the humanity woven into each story.

*All the stories and photographs in the "Will You See Me?" project were recorded with the permission and signed authorization of the person represented. Each participant in the project received compensation for their time in the form of local retail gift cards.

As humans, we each have the capacity to be "difference-makers," to change the world in some profound way. I sincerely hope you become acquainted with each of the precious souls who are a part of this project. I hope that you, too, will not be left unchanged and that you'll share a smile and wave to the people who need to be seen.

We sincerely hope this collection of stories will move each of our hearts with compassion, and stir us to reconsider our perspective toward those we may have previously deemed insignificant. May we acknowledge our fellow sojourners in a spirit of dignity – especially that special someone we have the privilege to briefly encounter at a roadway intersection.

May we all be Difference Makers. It starts when we smile and say, "I see you."

Reverend Shawn Morrison, Author
Founder/Executive Director of Good in the 'Hood

Shawn Nielsen, Photographer/Author
Owner of Nielsen Studios

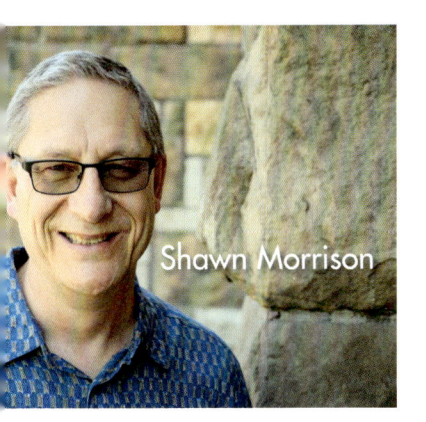

WE INVITE YOU TO 'SEE' MORE!

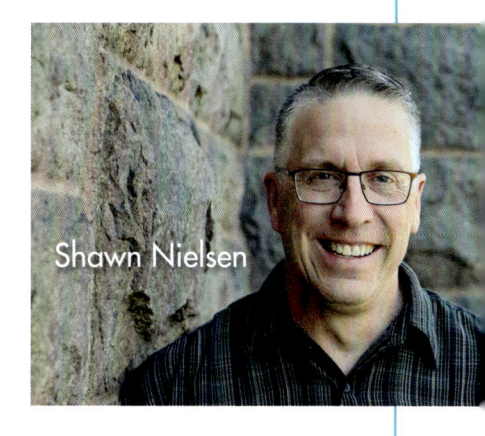

Shawn Morrison

Shawn Nielsen

We would love to share more about the people we met, the stories they shared, and the lessons we have learned along the way. To learn more about this important project, to order a copy of "Will You See Me?," or to invite us to come and share with your group, please visit our website by scanning the QR code or using the link: willyouseeme.com

To directly connect with Shawn Morrison and/or Shawn Nielsen or invite us to share with your group, please email us at shawn@goodinthehood.org. We would love to hear from you.

Preface

The late Mother Teresa was sometimes known as "The Saint of the Gutters" for her humble work with the poor, the disregarded, the frail, and the unhoused. During her lifetime of service to humanity, she inspired countless others by her tender and caring devotion to those Jesus referred to as "the least of these." She famously said, "Peace begins with a smile," and, "If you judge people, you have no time to love them." These same sentiments sit at the heart of what has compelled us to compile these interviews into a book called "Will You See Me?"

From the outset, we have endeavored to serve as advocates—to help give a voice to the unheard and a face to the unseen. We hope to offer a platform for our neighbors in need to share another side of their story and gently remind all of us to always treat others humanely, regardless of whether we agree with what they do to survive.

In capturing these exclusive stories, it is not necessarily our intent to exonerate those who panhandle to support their existence, nor are we looking to vilify them. Rather, we want to provide our participants with an opportunity to share their story in their own words and in their own chosen space. We trust these uniquely personal accounts will serve to inform our collective compassion and to soften our cynicism.

There are several layers of intentionality woven into the production of this book. This includes the physical manner in which we've chosen to present these valuable stories. Rather than a less expensive glue-bound paperback style, we intentionally chose a hardcover book with stitched binding. This "covering of the stories" is done in the spirit of another well-known story found in the Christian gospels.* It's the account of a destitute son who has made poor choices in life. This "prodigal son" squanders an early inheritance. He reproaches the family name with corrupt choices and completely abandons his family relationships. He shows no respect or regard for his father (a metaphor for our heavenly Father) or his own kin. Eventually, this wayward son becomes penniless and is reduced to eating the food given to pigs. Emotionally broken and physically desperate, he comes to his senses and decides he must return home. By this time, his confidence is lost, he is suffocating in shame, and his entire self-image has been reduced to almost nothing. He considers himself as "no longer worthy to be called son." Feeling undeserving of his heritage, he simply hopes his dad might withhold his rejection and possibly offer him some residual kindness, or the table scrap leftovers sometimes given to a servant. What he does not account for is the unrestrained love of his father so lavishly poured out upon him.

Upon hearing of his lost son's return, the father rushes out to meet him, running with abandon. No judgment. No scolding. Just pure joy, love, and acceptance. With kind tenderness, the father wraps his travel-weary son in his very best robe.

For us, a hardcover book with stitched binding, and indeed, the care with which we have approached every other aspect of this project, is our version of bestowing love, acceptance, and our very "best robe." It's our way of covering these lost sons and daughters in a "robe of dignity," regardless of their past failures and mistakes.

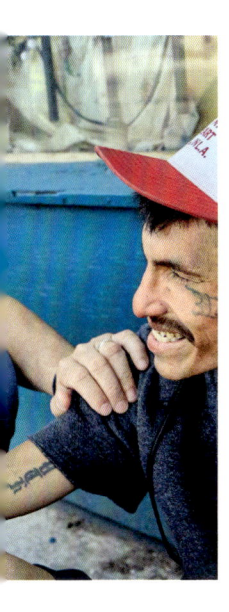

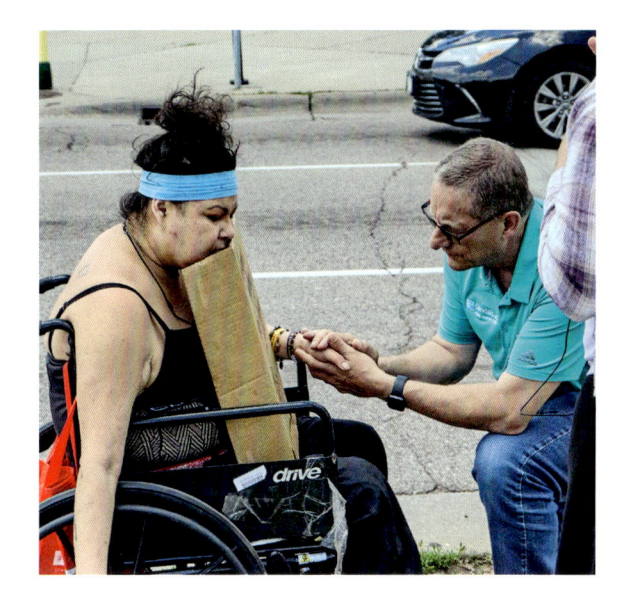

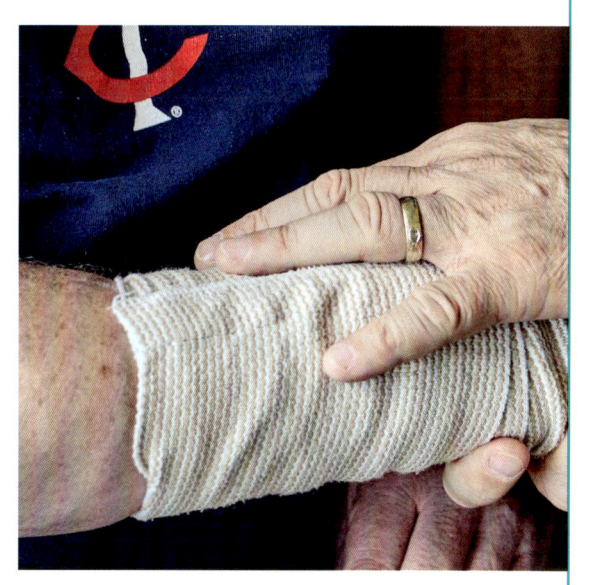

They may often feel like insignificant people, deserving only of life's scraps, but hopefully not today, and hopefully not in this book. These are human beings, just like each one of us. According to the Psalmist, one day, these poor and destitute ones will be raised from the "dunghill" of life to sit with the princes.

— Reverend Shawn Morrison, Author, *Founder and Executive Director of Good in the 'Hood*

PSALM 113:7-8 (KJV)

⁷ HE raiseth up the poor out of the dust, and lifteth the needy out of the dunghill;
⁸ That HE may set him with princes, even with the princes of HIS people.

*This parable told by Jesus is recorded in the book of Luke, chapter 15, verses 11-32.

Acknowledgments with Gratitude

Reverend Jamie Morrison
Director of Operations/Human Resources for Good in the 'Hood (booksbythebundle.com). Founder/CEO of Books by the Bundle.

My (Shawn Morrison's) beloved partner in life, who has been my most loyal companion and a constant source of inspiration and encouragement. Your labor of love and intuitive expertise to help review and edit this book has been priceless. Thank you for believing in this project and for believing in me. Most importantly, thank you for your faithful prayers and faith in our Lord. It's been wonderful journeying this life with you. You have all my love forever!

Jim Lingenfelter
Founder/CEO of Ignition Creative Solutions (ignitioncreativesolutions.com)

Your generosity and talent in providing the cover and interior design are nothing short of amazing. WOW! We are humbled by your kind investment in this important project. We are forever grateful for your willingness to give such high-level design talent to help us illuminate the lives of the overlooked. Thank you for caring and giving your best to support "the least of these."

Scott Whitman
Founder/CEO of Marketing With Insight (mwicomgroup.com), writer/editor, and content producer.

Your belief in this project, your expert advice, coaching, and professional editing support provided the wind in our sails that we needed to see this through to completion. Thank you for standing with us and helping us to position these narratives in a manner that authentically highlights our beloved subjects with compassion and dignity. Your gracious and patient coaching and your kind friendship mean so much to us. Thank you for sacrificially leaning in!

Elizabeth (Beth) Korth
Founder/Owner of Narrative Nuance (narrativenuance.com).

Thank you for your kind friendship and support for this initiative. You willingly jumped in and graciously interacted with each of our beloved participants by offering them a caring, personal touch. Thank you for treating each person with dignity as you successfully captured an audio recording of our conversations. You made our team better and we are truly grateful for your good heart.

Good in the 'Hood
A special thank you to our Board of Directors and staff, volunteers, stakeholders, and partners. This collection of stories is the fruit of our collective efforts to bring help and inspire hope to all those in need. This book and ministry would not be possible without your loving prayers, strong support, and wise guidance. Thank you for walking this journey with us. Together we are better!

'Will You See Me?' Participants
Finally, we offer a special "thank you" to the individuals whose stories and images are featured in this book. You are the MOST important people in this project. This undertaking is only made possible because of you. Your willingness to generously and courageously share your personal journey has enabled us to see another side of the far-too-often overlooked human story. We trust that these valuable life stories will inspire us all to treat everyone as a unique someone, to act more humanely, and help foster in us a spirit of intentional kindness toward everyone.

Good in the 'Hood — *Parent Organization*

BOOKS BY THE BUNDLE — *Publisher of "Will You See Me?"*

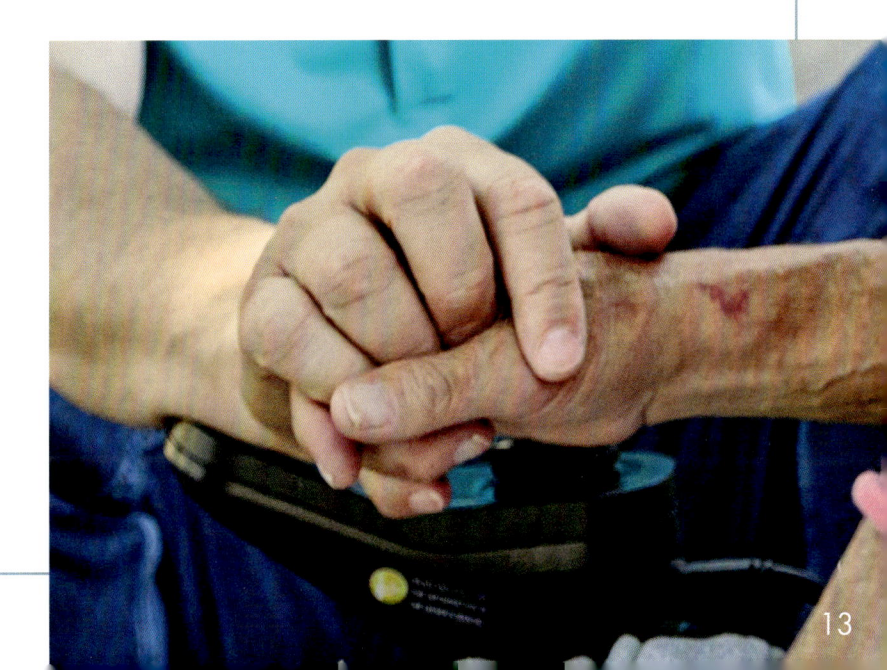

Alicia B.

Things aren't always as they seem. This is undoubtedly the case with Alicia, a youthful-looking 45-year-old with many scars, but not the kind of scars one can easily see. Her bubbly demeanor masks a life full of painful experiences. Hers is a story of one who doesn't easily give up. Distressful memories and disappointment etch deep scars within her soul. Yet, she is still here. She is still moving forward. And she still maintains a trust in God's divine goodness.

"Growing up in my neighborhood, things don't work out how you want them to."

Alicia's name means nobility. It seems fitting. She carries herself well and does not appear to be the stereotypical unhoused person from our curbside view: no unwashed, matted hair or unkempt clothing. Alicia does not give the appearance of hopelessness, nor does she wallow in a mindset of helplessness. She does not play the victim or pitch the kind of self-pitying narrative you might expect from someone who's walked her difficult path. No, Alicia is the opposite of everything most of us imagine when we envision someone living on the streets.

You see, Alicia is a glass-half-full person. She refuses to be defined by the circumstances of her life, regardless of how devastating. Although she lacks certain tools of privilege and opportunity, she humbly holds her head high, confident that she has better days ahead.

Born and raised in Chicago, Illinois, Alicia had to grow up sooner than anyone should. "I had my first child when I was 14. So, life happened to me really early. I've been a parent for a long time," she confided. Clearly, this was not an easy way to enter adolescence. One can only imagine how much easier life may have been for Alicia had she taken a different path. But she didn't. So, she did her best to navigate life as a young person forced to grow up much too soon.

15

In telling her story, Alicia reflected back on her youth – a time when she had a heart full of hopes and dreams that swirled within her soul like a kaleidoscope. "I wanted to be a lawyer… because I was really smart in school and a really good critical thinker." Those dreams painted her world with the vibrant hues of possibility that so often color the teenage soul. Unfortunately, Alicia's reality didn't match her imagined future. "Growing up in my neighborhood, things don't work out how you want them to," she lamented.

As the years unfurled before Alicia, life stubbornly refused to offer any respite. "I've always had issues with my mental health since I was 19 years old. Domestic abuse, health concerns, and mental health issues. I'm a diabetic." For Alicia, it's been a steep uphill climb to find stability.

"I'M STILL HERE. I didn't lose my feet. I'll give you that. I didn't lose my toes, so I count my blessings."

At 25, Alicia moved to Minneapolis, Minnesota, driven by a job opportunity. Since then, she has tackled various roles, from banking to dental care. Despite facing life's hurdles and personal struggles, maintaining steady work has proven challenging for her.

Surviving a recent near-tragic battle with the bitter cold winter elements brings Alicia's optimism into sharp focus. "I was frostbitten in January, and my feet were really bad. I was in the hospital for a month. But God is good. "I'M STILL HERE. I didn't lose my feet. I'll give you that. I didn't lose my toes, so I count my blessings."

Amazed by her story, we inquired about Alicia's family, goals, and current support system. "As far as a goal of mine... Getting my health back in order so that, hopefully, I can get back in the workforce before it's too late for me." Alicia's ultimate ambition is clear: "To get my mental health in order. I have terrible anxiety and PTSD. I can write a book (on my life story). I have been shot, I have been stabbed, and I had a baby when I was only 14. I have a lot of challenges."

As we bid farewell to Alicia, enveloping her in a heartfelt embrace, we extended an offer to pray together. Her response was resolute, accompanied by that familiar, captivating smile we had come to anticipate, "I DEFINITELY would take it! Thank you for listening."

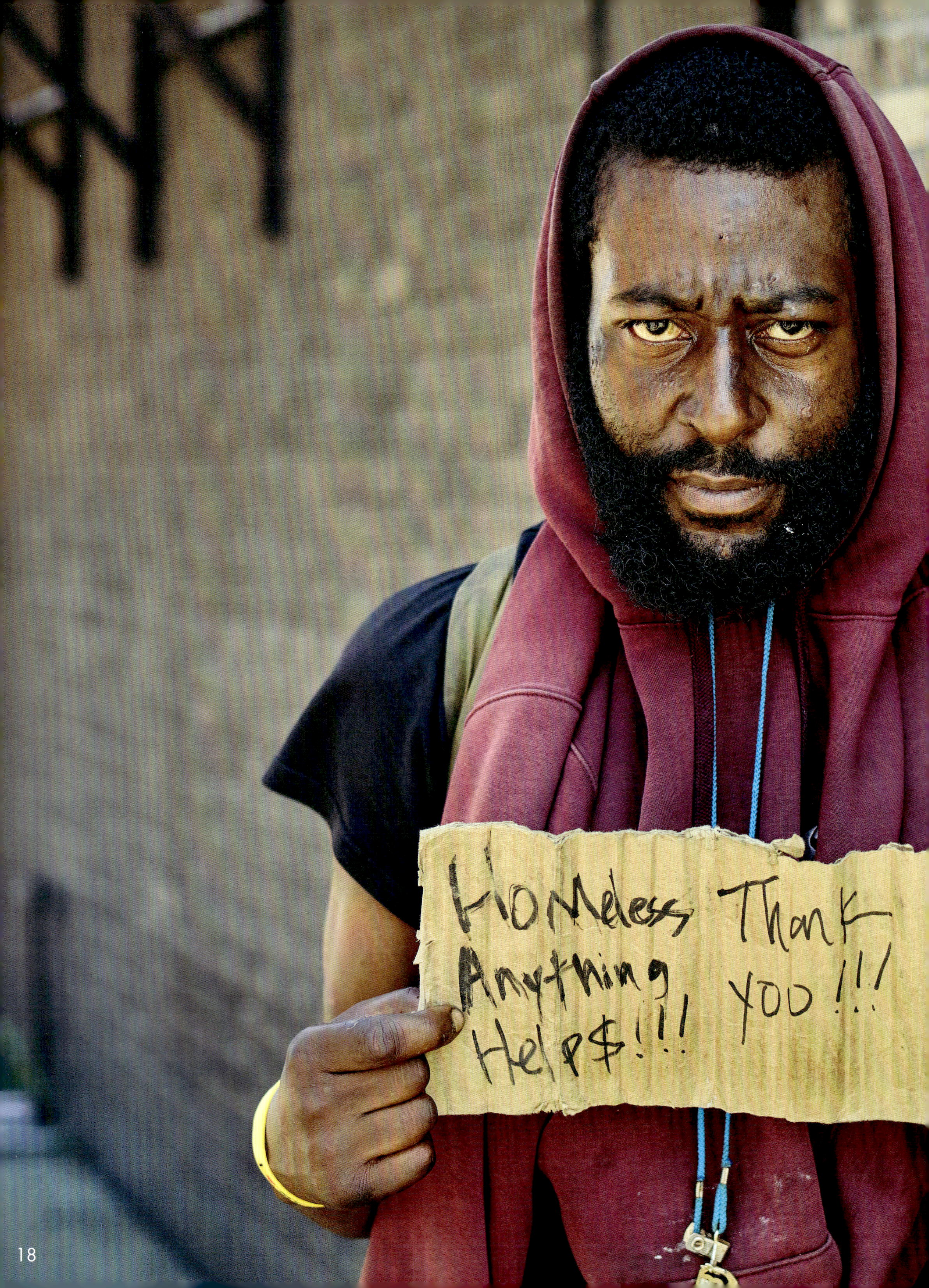
Homeless Thank
Anything you!!!
Help$!!!

Adrian J.

Adrian approached us somewhat intrusively as we were finishing a conversation with another person. Despite our reservations about his suitability as our target demographic, he asserted, "I am that demographic." At his insistence, we decided to proceed with the interview.

Adrian is an intelligent and quick-witted individual. He completed his college education and claims to hold a degree in business management but chose not to pursue a professional career. "It simply did not work out, primarily due to the environment. It was not a good fit," he explains.

Although Adrian is not currently employed in business management, he is industrious. Sign-flying is not his sole occupation. "Yeah, I do actual physical labor and work for people, contract work and carpentry and all that kind of stuff, but it's more sporadic. It's consistent, so I work. Again, sometimes you got to freestyle, you know what I mean? Sometimes you got to decide what you're going to do on the fly."

Adrian spent most of his childhood in North Minneapolis but experienced a transient upbringing. "We moved around, you know, place to place. And I kind of, you know, just decided to venture off on my own. I don't like a lot of, you know, I guess dependence. So that's basically why I ended up out here."

His parents are still alive and together, though he only sees them occasionally. He also has a brother with whom he does not maintain regular contact. "As I mentioned, I prefer not to rely on others for certain matters. When I am in someone else's home, I must adhere to their rules. Sometimes, I do not appreciate too many rules," he remarks with a slight, mischievous smile.

Adrian refuses to be defined by certain societal norms. "My skill set is whatever. I do whatever I need to do." Moreover, Adrian doesn't let his lack of an address impact his money-making efforts. "It's hard to get work and hard to be consistent with organizing and scheduling and all that stuff, but you just got to make it work."

"I am that demographic."

Adrian's responses reflect a certain practicality and a dash of wry wit. Asked how he would get from place to place, he muttered dryly, "Bus…just like everybody else." When asked if he sleeps on the ground or a blanket, he retorted, "No, I have a mattress like everyone else."

While theft can be a harsh reality on the streets, Adrian has a pragmatic view. "Yeah, that's in every walk of life. People just steal." Surprisingly, he eschews permanent housing, countering, "No permanent house, no permanent mortgage, no permanent rent," and added, "And there are no bills either."

Adrian prefers a basic lifestyle without attachments or a need for storage. "I don't need much to survive. Just my bag."

Although Adrian's path to his simple life on the street may be unique, his experiences with public disapproval are all too familiar. "The hardest part is people judging. Their actions, words, and body language—all sorts of weird stuff. But that's for them and God to sort out."

Like most of us, Adrian wants to be treated with respect and dignity.

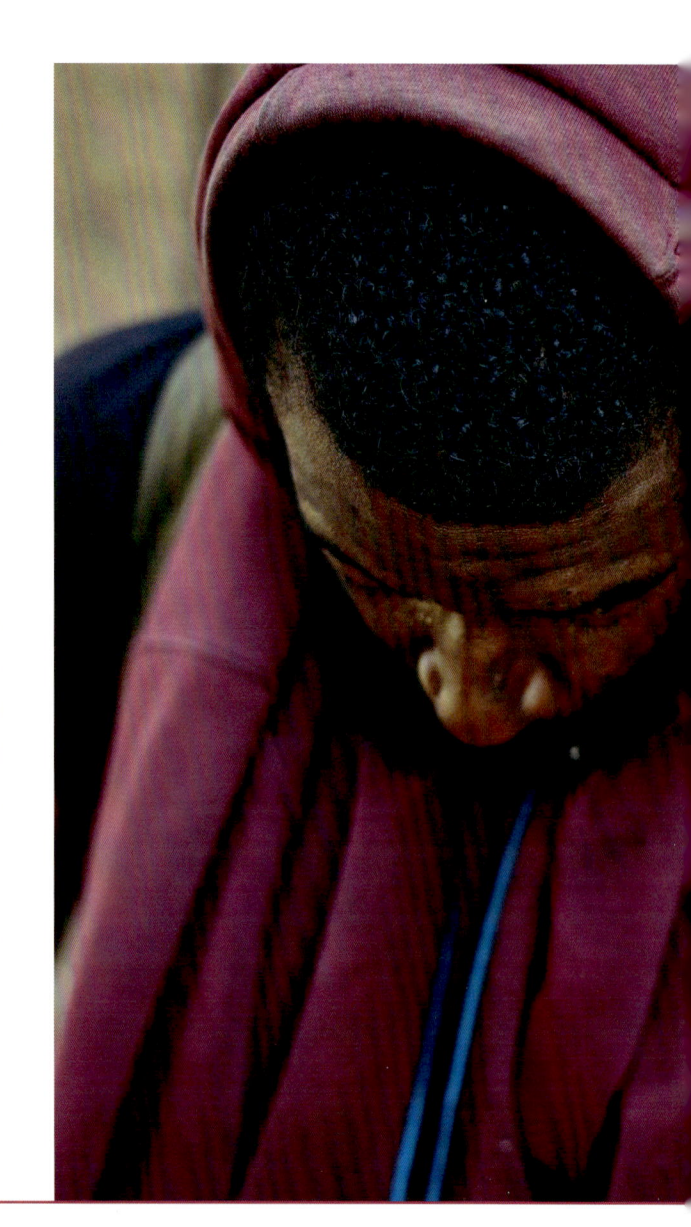

"Just approach everybody with the same respect you'd want. Everybody pretty much has the same desires, the same wants. And, you know, I'm no different than any other person"

"Just some thoughtfulness, maybe, you know? It doesn't have to be much. Just approach everybody with the same respect you'd want. Everybody pretty much has the same desires, the same wants. And, you know, I'm no different than any other person walking in that Taco Bell or Wendy's or, you know, I got to eat, I got to drink, I got to use the bathroom, I got to sit down, I got to take a load off, I got to relax, I got to work, I got to do all that same stuff everybody else has to do."

Adrian's future goals are straightforward and considerate of others. "I'm always happy with what I'm doing, but I just want to see everybody be happy with what they're doing, so…that's about it."

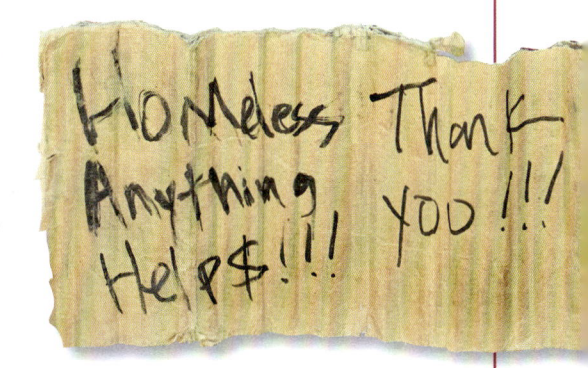

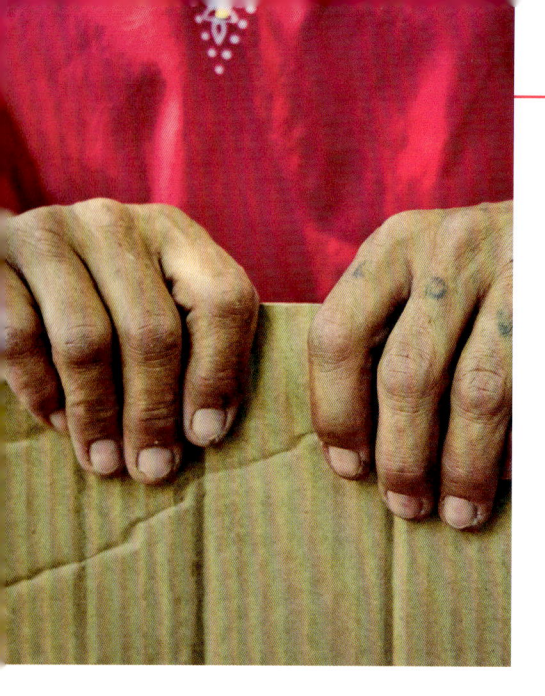

Alison K.

Wearing a bright pink dress and green sneakers, Alison displays a tender strength and a calming presence. Despite sitting in a wheelchair, she emanates an energy for life and a generous joy. She is one of the sweetest people one might have the pleasure of meeting. But it hasn't always been this way for Alison. She's had hard times too. Alison's faith and the kindness she has experienced from others is what she treasures in her heart and inspires her most.

Originally from Rhinelander, Wisconsin, Alison has lived a lifetime filled with countless challenges. Alison's parents were divorced when she was only 12, but she says, "Life was better that way." At the tender age of 15, Alison became a mom, leaving behind the carefree days of youth and shelving her childhood aspirations. Her sole focus became excelling at this important new role in life. "I just wanted to be a good mom," she confided. Although Alison never married she shared, "Well, I mean, I had like an 11-year relationship. It was kind of a common law thing. You know, so, no actual ceremony." Sadly this relationship ended leaving her to manage life and the children on her own. Presently, she cherishes her role as "Mom" to two daughters and a son, and "Grandma" to two grandchildren.

Both of her parents are deceased. Her father was a Marine and died "from drinking" when he was only 42. Just a few years ago, she lost her mother to "smoking." The weight of life without her beloved mother hit hard. Tears well up in her eyes as she confides, "She was my best friend."

23

"...we're people too. I've been on both ends. And if you can't help, or you don't want to... You don't have to say negative things or do negative things."

Several years ago, with the support of the Salvation Army and through what Alison perceives as divine intervention, she found herself in Minnesota. "I was in a meth bust back when I was in Rhinelander. I was under a no-contact mandate with my 12 closest friends. So, when I got out of jail, I didn't have anywhere to go." Feeling useless, aimless, and disposable, Alison knew she had to make some serious changes.

This led her to a rehab facility in Wausau, Wisconsin, where her battle with substance abuse persisted. "I had gone to every treatment that Wisconsin would take my insurance card for. And so, I ended up coming here to the Salvation Army. And it was a 30-day program. It took me seven months. I got out, and I started building a relationship with God. And I went to church."

Disabled and Dismissed

Sometimes, one can do everything right, and life can still take a tragic turn. After having turned her life around, Alison suffered a terrible health scare. "One day, I went to sleep and woke up three weeks later from a coma. And I couldn't move anything from the waist down. I was sober. I was going to church. I had spinal meningitis. The doctor said, 'It was the luck of the draw.'" This unexpected illness has left Alison with significant mobility issues and the need to depend upon a walker and a wheelchair to get around.

Having mobility issues makes everyday tasks far more burdensome for Alison. This is something she expected. What Alison didn't anticipate was how terrible some people treat her because of her disability. Because she is disabled, she is also frequently dismissed. Yet, like each one of us, she longs for nothing more than to be treated humanely and with dignity.

Alison has limited housing options and must reside in a rundown apartment complex. "This is the worst place to live. They just moved me into an apartment. But the guy was totally unkind to me. And they hadn't cleaned it at all. I have a housing worker who's helping me right now." She breaks down in tears; the weight of her situation is an obvious burden. "I just want to keep a home where, you know, my grandkids can come to see me."

Once Alison regains her composure, we ask her what she would like to share with those who are critical of those who panhandle for a living. She softly whispers, "Just that we're people too. I've been on both ends, you know. And if you can't help, or you don't want to... You don't have to say negative things or do negative things."

While tears were shed, there was also gratitude. As we wrap up with a few closing questions, we ask Alison if there is anyone who has profoundly impacted her life. She answers, "The envoys and, you know, the people at the Salvation Army in Wausau who sent me here. You know, they could have thrown me back out on the streets, but they didn't."

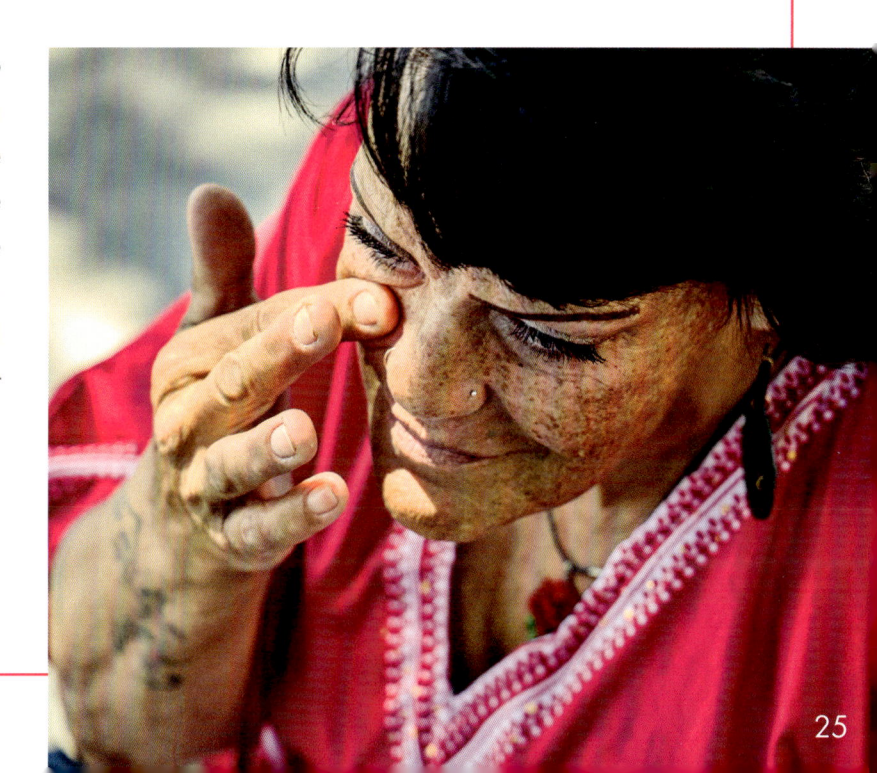

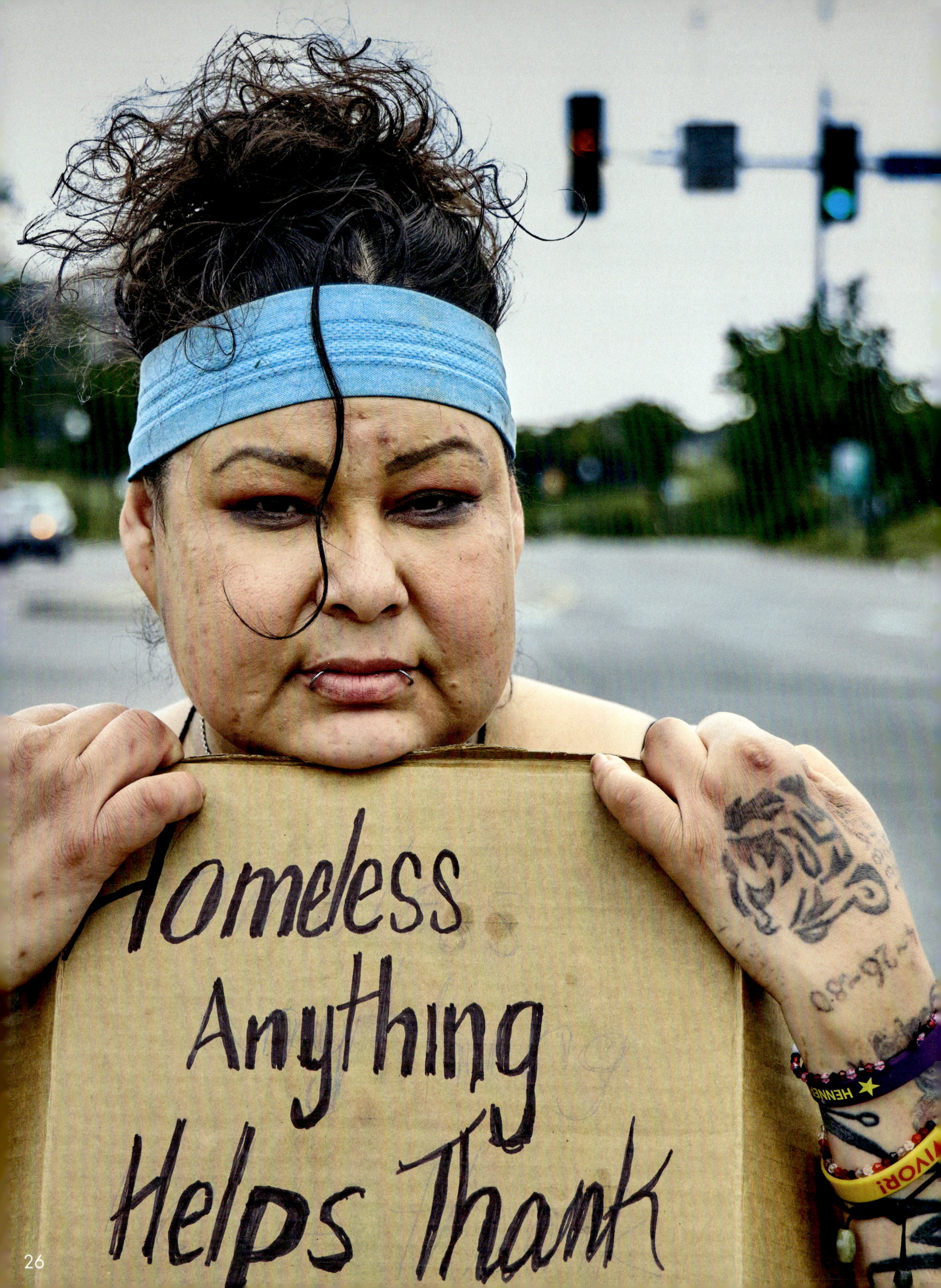
Homeless
Anything
Helps Thank

Adrianne M.

On the frenetic intersection of Cedar and Franklin Avenue in South Minneapolis, we meet Adrianne, a middle-aged Native American woman navigating life with resilience and grace. Adrianne's story is one of immense struggle and tenacity, a narrative that humbles us and beckons us to listen, learn and act.

Listening to Adrianne and learning about her story was a noteworthy experience and a gift to our collective souls.

Adrianne's life has been anything but easy. Panhandling at a South Minneapolis corner with her 13-year-old daughter, Precious Adrianne hustles to make a few dollars, a testament to her daily harsh realities. Adrianne lives in a wheelchair, having recently adapted to a prosthetic leg. Her lower lip adorned with two ornate rings, and her dark, curly hair held up by a bright blue band. She presents a striking figure. A bracelet on her wrist boldly declares in red lettering, "A Survivor" – a not-so-subtle indicator of what she has overcome.

As we prepare to speak with Adrianne, Precious sits patiently on the narrow grassy median, ready to spring into action whenever a sympathetic motorist offers a bit of monetary charity. Observing this family dynamic, we can't help but wonder, "What brought them here?" and "What is their story?" Little did we know how compelling and heart-wrenching it would be.

"...to get a job, I need a place, and in order to get a place, I need a job."

Adrianne's Pathway

Adrianne's formative years were spent with a foster parent on the Leech Lake reservation. Her childhood was marked by academic brilliance and the rejection that comes with being seen by her classmates as a teacher's pet. Despite not having any close friends, Adrianne excelled in her studies, graduating early and pursuing post-secondary education before age 15. Sadly, tragedy unexpectedly struck, "My foster parent died when I was 15. So, instead of going to another home, I ran away and came here. Growing up on the Rez is a whole different life. You have to grow up on your own anyway. And I was a little bit scared. That's why I ran away."

Without the typical parental guidance or a stable support system, life became a series of struggles for Adrianne. She briefly found stability working as a licensed care assistant for a dialysis nurse, but her world was shattered once again when she lost her first baby. "I was young, and I got pregnant at 19 with my first baby. He passed away." The loss affected Adrianne's emotional well-being and drove her into unhealthy and abusive relationships. Struggling to regain stability, Adrianne had more children, which further compounded her difficulties as a young single mother.

Despite these struggles, Adrianne's resilience is evident as she shares her story. "I was married for five years. I got divorced last year. I lost my finger and my leg when he tried to kill me in a car accident."

Now, Adrianne faces the daily grind of survival, panhandling to feed herself and her children. Her two younger children, ages 9 and 5, are in daycare while she and Precious labor for a bit of meal money. Despite her circumstances, Adrianne's dreams for the future remain vivid. "I wanted to have some independence, make a living, and be able to see the world. I just wanted to be able to travel. I also wanted to have my own business…a restaurant. The name was gonna be P-Dubs, short for Pow Wows."

Dreams, no matter how vivid, must wait as the urgent matter of navigating everyday life – like where she will sleep tonight – occupies her thoughts. Couch-hopping has become Adrianne's best option, though it's not always available. "You get used to it. I've been doing it my whole life." She struggles to make enough to feed herself and her children, earning only about $10 an hour waving signs at street corners. Her life has been reduced to "Trying to make it to the next day. I know where my kids can sleep, but just because they can sleep with friends doesn't mean I can. I just want my kids to do better than I did."

When asked how people can help, aside from giving money, without hesitation, Adrianne asks that anyone who might meet her on a corner, "Not to be so judgmental. It's like when people drive by here, and they sit; they'll mess with everything in their car to avoid looking at us. If they were to offer me a job that I could do. I mean, I can do anything. I just might need a little longer, but I can still do things now that I got this prosthetic leg. I'm still learning how to walk. It's harder, but I need just a little bit of time. I can still work with a cash register. I can still count money. I can still make phone calls. But to get a job, I need a place, and in order to get a place, I need a job."

As we listen to Adrianne's story, we are struck by her strength and resolve to continue pressing forward. Her journey is a poignant reminder of the importance of compassion for the vulnerable.

Let us rediscover the bond of humanity in every individual we encounter. By doing so, we will uplift others and enrich our own lives, and through that discovery, we can foster a better, more compassionate society.

Bentrell H.

Irony can offer some interesting and strange twists. As we visit Bentrell (Ben) Howze, it's hard to miss the peculiarity of his surname. His last name, pronounced much like "house," serves as a cruel, relentless reminder of his perpetual search for a permanent place to anchor his weary soul. Sadly, Ben seems tethered to the hopelessness of the unforgiving streets. Even the T-shirt hanging on his weary frame, boldly declaring "CASHMAKER," testifies to the ineffectiveness of the claim by one in such a cash-poor and destitute position.

> **"That's what they (our parents) don't understand. They went through childhood. They were young and dumb, too. You know what I mean? Let us take our turn."**

On this warm and sunny late July morning, Ben has an I-just-rolled-out-of-bed appearance. Standing on the median with a cardboard sign that has been rewritten multiple times, he projects little expectation that anyone will take the time to read it. Upon approaching and introducing ourselves, Ben agrees to move across the street to a quieter space for a conversation. He is congenial and carefree. Occasionally yawning and casually rubbing his head as if to clear the morning cobwebs from his brain.

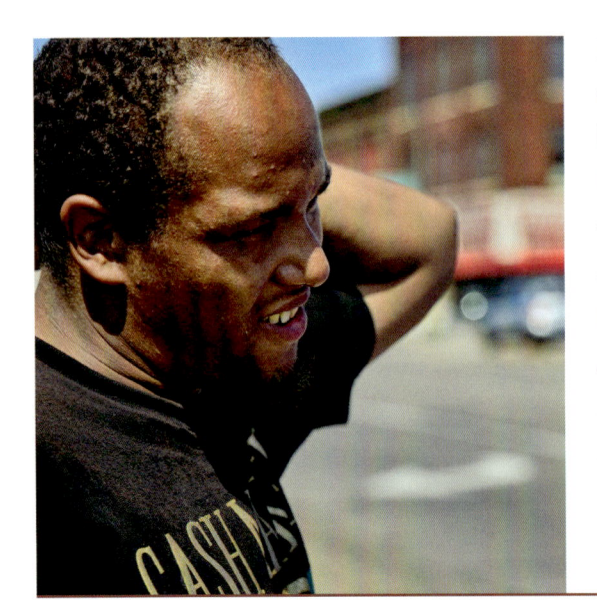

Ben wears his shoes in a slipshod manner, with the heel folded under his soles. He tilts his head back to enjoy the final few puffs of his smoke, noticeably finding satisfaction with the long, drawn-out final drags. As we continue our interchange on the ever-busy Broadway Avenue, near a North Minneapolis encampment, he is carefully scanning the area, acutely aware of all those who are moving around us.

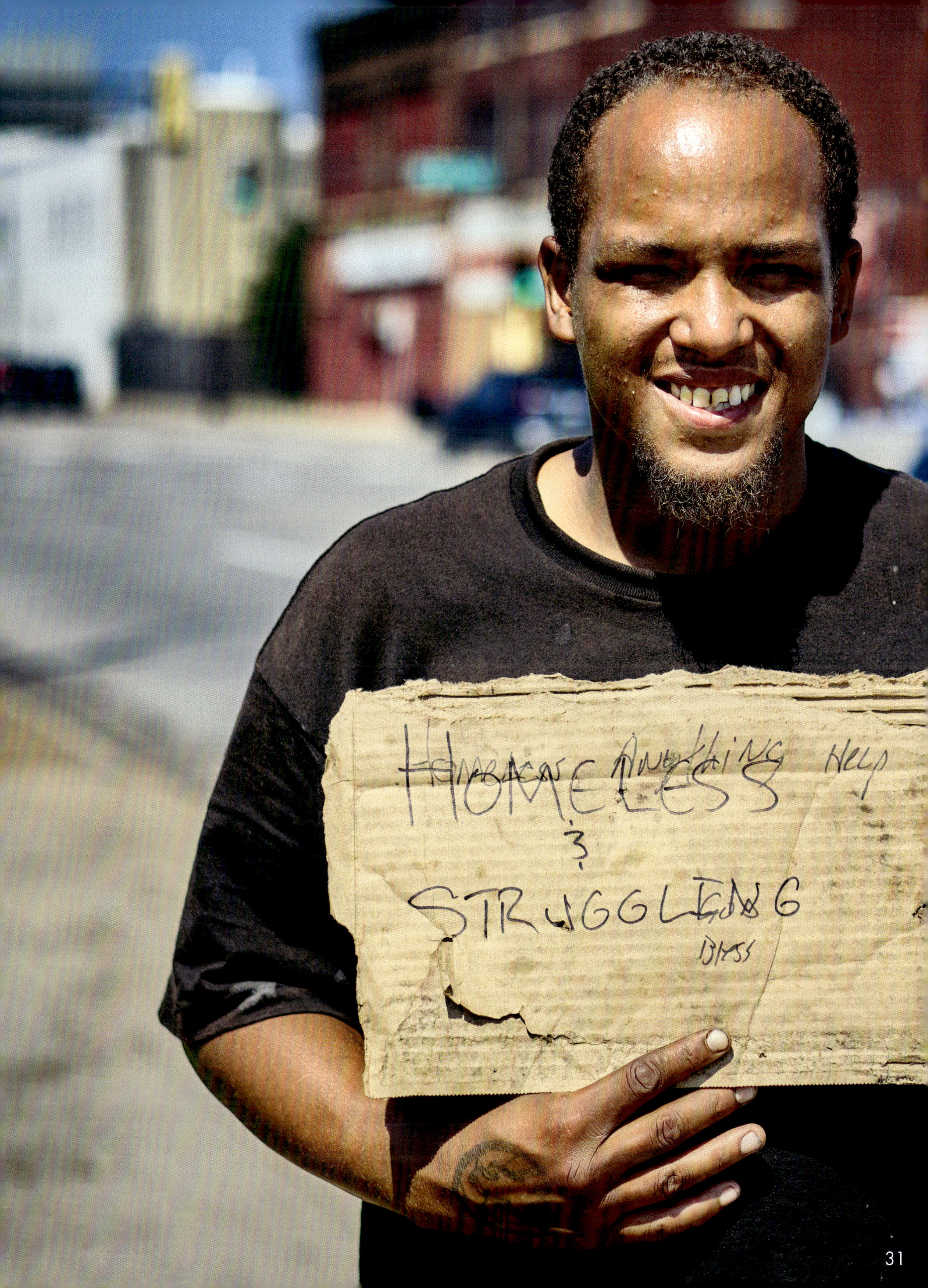
Help
HOMELESS
&
STRUGGLING

There is a certain incongruity, however, as his manner seems both relaxed and attentively distracted. Nodding towards a resident from the nearby encampment, he says, "I'm just waiting for someone to creep up on my spot. Like, if he was to go on my spot right now, I'd go down to the next one, you know?" Clearly his "spot" is a prime piece of real estate. It's all about location when it comes to successful panhandling.

Throughout our poignant exchange, Ben bares his soul with unfiltered honesty. Every word raw and candid, devoid of facade or exaggeration, laying bare his tumultuous life's journey. He's in the moment, and our exchange flows nicely. At one point, he asked for a bottle of water, and we gladly accommodated him. Clearly dehydrated, he chugged down the entire bottle. His desperate thirst is a vivid reminder of the stress and challenges of life on the streets: no easy access to basic needs such as water, restrooms, or even a comfortable place to sit and rest. Loiterers are chased away. Finding a safe space to pause and give one's feet a brief respite is an ongoing struggle.

Ben grew up in the northern Minnesota Red Lake and Bemidji area. Asked about his early years, Ben shared, "I grew up in a single-mother home. Single mom with five kids. She was an alcoholic, so I kind of raised myself. All the others were grown when I was out of the household, so I really had no guidance. I wanted to be a police officer. I'm a felon now. Can't even hold a gun. That's really about it." Ben ended up in foster care near Nevis, Minnesota, at sixteen years old. He gratefully states, "I'm thankful I got to graduate because of foster care."

His transition to the Twin Cities was somewhat accidental. "My friend's daughter got into a car accident, and we came down here to the children's hospital. We got in a fight, and we were on the highway. I told him, I'll get out right here, and he stopped. I didn't think he was actually going to stop. I hopped out, and I walked all the way back to Minneapolis. So, that's what got me here, and then the drugs kept me, to be honest. I'm pretty blunt about it. I'm ready to be done with it. The drugs get me when I'm on the street."

Every Man for Himself

Ben waves his sign almost daily for "two hours every time, and then I leave, and then I come back." The best time is during "rush hour." We asked Ben how much he might make in a couple of hours. "Hopefully forty," he states. Water and food are also some practical basics he appreciates receiving. Depending upon the location and the time of day, there is money to be made. It's not a great living, but most will say, "It's tax-free," regardless of the legalities. It can be long hours facing the elements and having to throw one's self-esteem into the backseat. Ben chuckles as he tells us about taunts from the kind of person panhandlers refer to as a "Mustang Sally…The one that's like, 'Get a job,' and, like, all that s**t are difficult to deal with." Apparently, "Mustang Sally" is a slang name for people of privilege who drive by shouting obscenities and critical words at the sign-waving populace.

Ben is admittedly irresponsible and refreshingly honest about it. He's not dealing with any physical disabilities that prevent him from working. He's tired of spending his nights sleeping in bus stops. "I get it, I'm young and I'm able to work, but it's just not me yet. I got a lot of growing up to do, I would say. That's what they (our parents) don't understand. They went through childhood. They were young and dumb, too. You know what I mean? Let us take our turn. At first, I was embarrassed to do it. And then, I was like, you know what? It's better than robbing and stealing, so we might as well sit out here in the sun all day and make a little bit. Actually, I just got into AVIVO. I want to settle down again and begin doing hard labor jobs."

As our conversation comes to a close, we inquire about the presence of a supportive community in his life. "Yeah, kind of," he says. He reluctantly nods towards the tent community. "You can see them. It's kind of every man for himself, really."

34

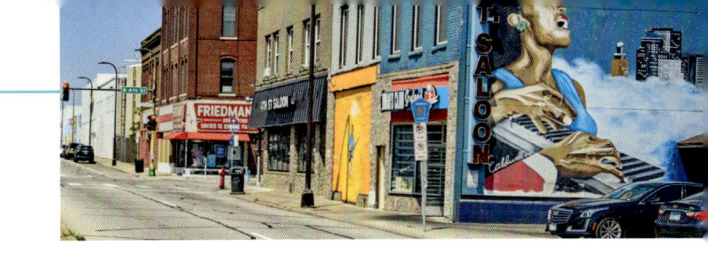

Brenda W.

At the West Broadway corridor in North Minneapolis, in the median next to the famous "Welcome To North Minneapolis" Billie Holliday mural, sits a woman in a wheelchair and a floppy straw hat with an endearing gap-toothed smile, her face shining as bright as the afternoon sun. Manning her curbside post, Brenda holds what appears to be a hastily made basic cardboard sign.

Brenda is easily approachable, and her charming countenance says, "Welcome," without ever having to utter a single word. With an obvious gift for spinning a yarn, she seems to pay no mind to the deafening traffic all around us as she captivates us with her story.

Born in Minneapolis, Brenda had a difficult upbringing. She recounts her own story so well, we enjoy the opportunity to mostly listen, interjecting only occasionally when we can manage to get in a word.

As a youth, "I ended up getting in a lot of trouble. And I basically ended up in prison by the time I was 18 years old. I was practically just out of diapers before I knew what I was doing, and I didn't know that the minute the judge sentenced me, I had wrecked my whole life."

This early conviction sentenced Brenda to a life facing hurdles her younger self could not have imagined. "When I got out of prison, they gave me $100 and told me, 'good luck.' I was twenty-two when they released me. And I'm supposed to start my life over. And I hadn't a clue. Couldn't get a job anywhere. Because of that question…'Have you ever been convicted of a felony?' And even now, people, they don't know what to think of ex-offenders and what to do with them. And so, you know, it's been a struggle working at the temp services. I ended up, because I had upper body strength and I was willing to work, they would send me to construction cleanup jobs. Digging pipe trenches."

"I went to Seattle in 1991. I heard about the fishing industry out there, so I decided I was going to go get on a boat." We asked if she enjoyed seafood. With a chuckle, she replied, "I did until I got on that boat. But I ended up basically homeless. I experienced homelessness for close to 20 years. I've been homeless here, homeless there, and couch surfing…was a whole different experience. And nobody knew me, and nobody cared about me, and it's like, how am I going to do this? I kept working at temp services, and we had a little drinking circle."

Brenda quickly transitioned from temporary and back-breaking jobs to panhandling, which proved to be much better for her body. "One Saturday, there was a guy out in Washington State, and he showed me how to wave signs. He said, 'We go out there and stand down on the corner and beg people for money.' He said, 'You're a woman. You'll do just fine.' And I said, 'Uh-uh.' He said, 'Try it.' So, I did. Went out there, was out there maybe eleven minutes, made me eleven dollars. And I said, 'S**t! That's a good idea. I'm going to sit there and make my money this way. Instead of working like a plow mule. And that was maybe 13 years ago."

"I'm just trying to do what I need to do. You know and stay positive through it… I still got a lot of living to live

Along the way, Brenda has encountered a few Good Samaritans to help her become reconnected with her three children. "I ran into these two ladies out in Portland, Oregon. They saw me with a broken leg outside of a department store with the same sign. And they came and asked me my story. So, I told them I followed somebody out here. We were supposed to be in love and all this. And I got stranded, and now I'm stuck. And they were like, 'Well, where are you from?' I told them I was from here (Minneapolis). They said, 'Do you want to see your family?' I said, 'Yeah, I've got family. I've got kids.' And they said, 'But you would like to see them again?' And I said, 'Yeah.' And so, they took me to the Greyhound, bought me a bus ticket. And I came home (Minneapolis) the next day."

As life continued to progress, Brenda received some very concerning news causing her to re-evaluate her lifestyle. "I ended up going to the doctor to get a physical. They found out I had hepatitis C. They told me that if I didn't stop drinking, I was going to die. So, I thought, okay, the party's over, but how am I going to do this? I mean, it was rough getting to sober up and to maintain sobriety."

"Why don't the world care about me? Well, the world didn't know me. I have to show the world who I am."

Brenda entered treatment to receive the support she needed to kick her habits. This opened her up to her faith roots, which have become the all-important catalyst for Brenda to live her life with significance. "When I first went into AA, I was in treatment. And my family are deep into the Christian faith. And they were like, okay, when the people start talking to you about a higher power, then you'll understand exactly where we're at mentally and emotionally. I didn't realize that our higher power has a personal relationship with each of us."

Following treatment, Brenda had a very discouraging reality check. "I went back to college, the first two years, I was studying to become a Chemical Dependency counselor. I got to the end of everything, but before you make the transition into being a counselor, you have to go through an internship and a background check. They did my background check, and the state of Minnesota said never ever could I work as a counselor. That disillusioned me real bad. So, what am I supposed to do? I've been trying to figure out what am I supposed to do? And maybe it's just to be empathic and be as helpful of a person as I can. I can't do much, but just to sometimes have a good conversation with a person. Or help them."

Brenda's heart is alive and vibrant with a great love for God and for others. Unfortunately, her body is aging somewhat prematurely, from years of abuse and working physically demanding jobs. "In my head, I'm not 63 years old." She has muscle contractions in her hips, knees, and ankles. "They told me that by doing all that work, I had caused a ruptured disc in my spine and all kinds of stuff that I didn't know I had. I'm just finding all this stuff out in the last year. Just had back surgery last year. I had an apartment downtown that I had to get rid of because of all of this. And now, I'm just trying to do what I need to do. You know, and stay positive through it. And so now today… I'm in a nursing home. With $125 a month allowance. So, not enough to do anything."

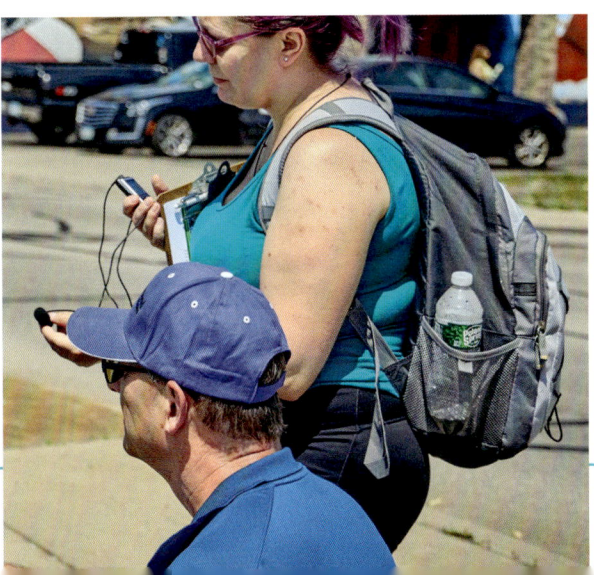

With little regular income and no capacity to work a regular job, Brenda resorts to panhandling to make ends meet. On occasion, she encounters someone who doesn't share her belief that panhandling is a legitimate source of income. "The people that say nasty things and try to be mean to people that are out here…they are miserable. People that look at me holding up this sign, they may say, 'Go get a job!'… I can't get no job, not really, especially now. But I'm grateful to be a believer; I'm grateful to be able to at least try to do something for myself. I still got a lot of living to live. I got grandchildren that I haven't finished spoiling yet. My kids don't like that I'm out here. But like I said, if you aren't doing anything to take care of me, at least let me take care of myself."

As we began to wrap up our time with Brenda, she offered a few final words straight from her heart. "People try to dehumanize people in these situations, but it's up to me whether I'm going to take that on. They can call me a homeless bum or whatever, and it's like, I know that these people don't know what my situation is. So, for them to judge me because I'm out here, I just have to ignore that. Nobody wants to be out here. Nobody said when they were a little kid that they wanted to grow up to be a raging junkie. Nobody wants that. There's trauma all over these places. The people that you talk to, most of them have been through one trauma or another. I've had some personal trauma in my life, too. I had to get over it and just keep going. Don't get me started saying, 'Poor me. Why don't the world care about me?' Well, the world didn't know me. I have to show the world who I am. So, when I get an opportunity to talk to people like you, that's just what I do. I'm just appreciating the fact that you guys are out here trying to look out for me."

And it's nice to know that there are good people like Brenda who are looking out for others, too.

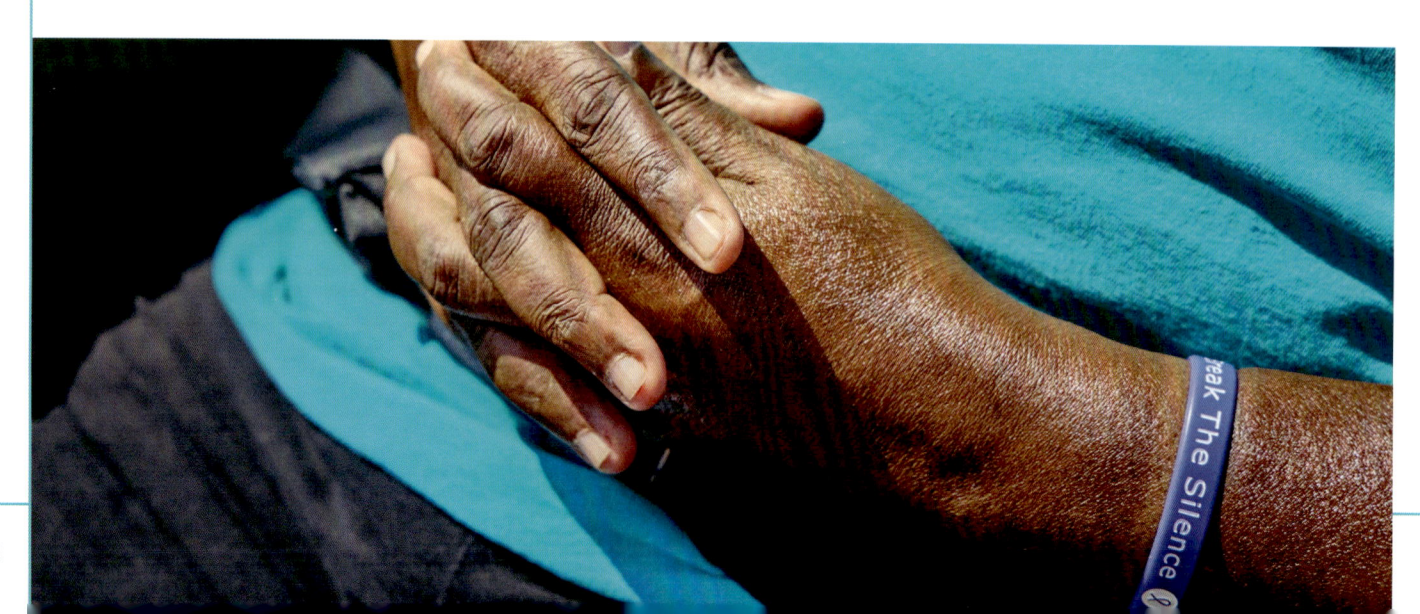

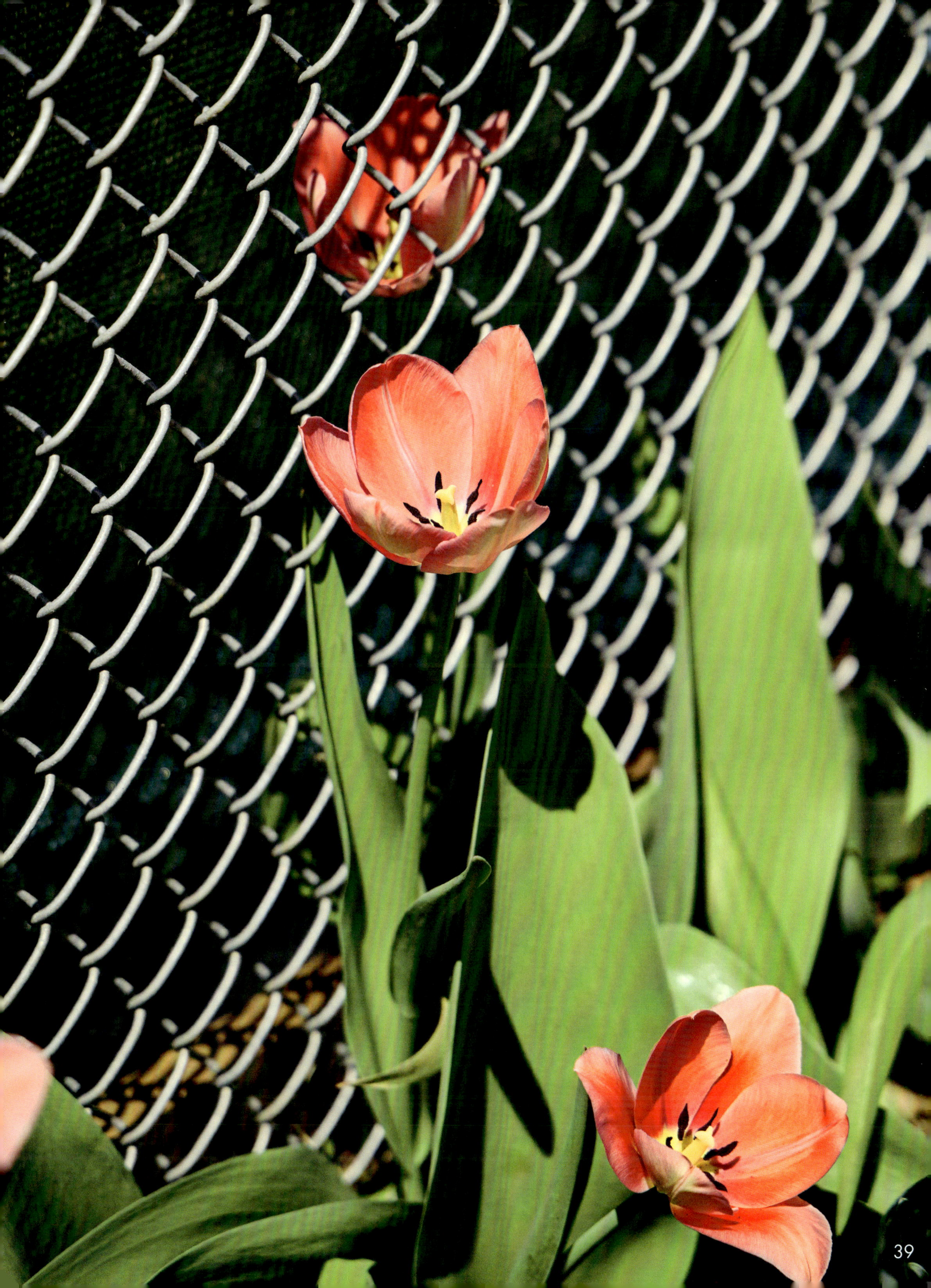

Christopher P.

It's a sunny summer afternoon, and Saint Paul, Minnesota, is all noise. Honking car horns, wailing sirens, the whoosh of the freeway traffic below us, and wind buffeting our ears. People screaming, music blaring. Sound is everywhere… loud, annoying, chaotic dissonance.

On any given day, with all of its noisy discord, this out-of-tune urban symphony can be nearly deafening, or at least it tempts one to put on a good set of noise-reduction headphones. Yet, seemingly unaffected by this inner-city pandemonium, a middle-aged man with a bald head and a silvery beard stands tall at the corner of a freeway off-ramp. Enthusiastically waving his cardboard sign, he radiates happiness toward passersby as if he's fervently embraced the role of self-appointed community ambassador. His infectious grin, though lacking some teeth, adds to his charm. Unperturbed by the chaos surrounding him, he exudes joy and dedicates himself to sharing it with all who cross his path.

American writer Elbert Hubbard once coined the phrase, "When life throws you lemons, make lemonade." It's a recipe for positivity and how to make the most out of our trials and challenges. It seems that Christopher, or Chris as he likes to be called, is someone who takes this to heart. He's formulating 'lemonade' as if he's working for a PhD in Optimism. Chris's love of life is contagious, and it feels good to be around him. His cardboard sign bears a lengthy message far exceeding a commuter's attention span and is uniquely devoid of any pleas for money or aid. Instead, Chris's sign radiates a simple, 'BE HAPPY. GOD BLESS,' message to the community. He intentionally spreads God's love in practical ways to all who pass by.

"Happy is what you do around other people – help others, don't worry about yourself."

I WISH THAT EVERYONE HAS A FUN
SUMMER A YEAR. PLEASE BE SAFE.
YOU WILL BE BLESSED BY GOD. HE
WOKE US. TODAY AND GOD TOLD US HOW
TO GET BY EVERYDAY. WE LOV GOD WITH
ALL OUR HEART AND TRUST IN HIM.
YOU CAN NOT GO WRONG.
HAVE A GREAT GOD BLESS YOU
NIGHT

Although one couldn't tell by looking at him, Chris has had a hard life. He confides, "My story is long. It has been filled with struggles and difficult times. But I knew from the start that I needed to be enthusiastic, eager, interested in others, and to learn from each other. I needed to connect with people." In May 2018, following his parents' passing, he boldly chose to relocate to Minnesota. Why here? "Because I love wolves. I love the state; it's beautiful. Florida is hot, very hot year-round."

His journey has been anything but smooth. Finding and holding jobs has been difficult. Despite being a skilled forklift operator and having spent most of his life stocking grocery store shelves, stable employment eludes him in his quest to provide for his family. "I have a 7-year-old daughter, and she lives in New Jersey. We stay connected through phone calls. She is so beautiful. She lives with her mom."

"Just be happy towards people."

This daily task of raising support for his daughter and his own survival are strong priorities for Chris. "I need money to survive, so I can save for rent and food and send money to my daughter for clothes and other things."

"When I get a house, my daughter will come to visit me. She wants to see me. Until then, I will continue sending monthly support to her. I love her."

His strong faith has carried Chris through these difficult seasons, and his circumstances have not shaken it. He wants to work so he can make a living. However, regardless of what happens, he maintains a posture of trust. "If they don't give me money, no worries, God will provide, and I'll get things later. I don't get angry or sad."

When asked what it means to be happy, Chris replied, "Happy is what you do around other people – help others, don't worry about yourself. Smile, cherish people, be glad that people have food and a place to rest. Don't worry about it. It's a beautiful day. God is happy with me." He went on to say, "Just be happy; if you don't have money, don't worry about it. Just be happy towards people."

Chris's journey has been a tumultuous one, marked by significant challenges – the loss of his parents, being separated from his daughter, relocating to a new state without any support system, experiencing homelessness and living in a shelter, and his inability to find or hold a job. None of this has diminished his faith, dimmed the light in his soul, or removed the contagiously joyful smile that covers his face. He is a kind, generous, and inspirational person.

Perhaps Chris's most significant hurdle is simple communication. In addition to his cardboard sign, he depends upon American Sign Language to communicate. You see, Chris has been profoundly deaf since birth.

As we neared the end of our conversation, I apologized for my rusty interview and communication skills as I found myself stumbling through our dialogue. Ever so gracious, Chris replied, "We are understanding each other, and I need more practice, too. We are the same."

Of course, living with deafness makes Chris's efforts towards stability a much steeper climb than it is for most other unhoused persons. Yet, he will not use his deafness as an excuse. Chris chooses to press forward with an unrelenting optimism.

He is currently enrolled in Technical College to learn a trade to find employment and a stable career. With such a can-do positivity, Chris seems nearly unstoppable. It's heart-warming to meet a curbside collector who is working hard to have a better life.

Chris has never heard an annoying car horn honk, a "Get a job" jeer, or the blaring music of a car stereo. His world is visual, and his eyes have seen both the disapproving looks of his commuter audience and the blessed smiles of those who are kind. Despite being unable to hear a sound, it's quite possible he has learned the rule of Saint Benedict, "to listen with the ear of your heart."

Perhaps, like Chris, we should all endeavor to listen more with our hearts.

"When one door of happiness closes, another opens; but often we look so long at the closed door that we do not see the one which has been opened for us."
— Helen Keller

"I am only one,
but still I am one.
I cannot do everything,
But still I can do
something;
and because I cannot
do everything
I will not refuse to do
something that I can do."

-Edward Everett Hale

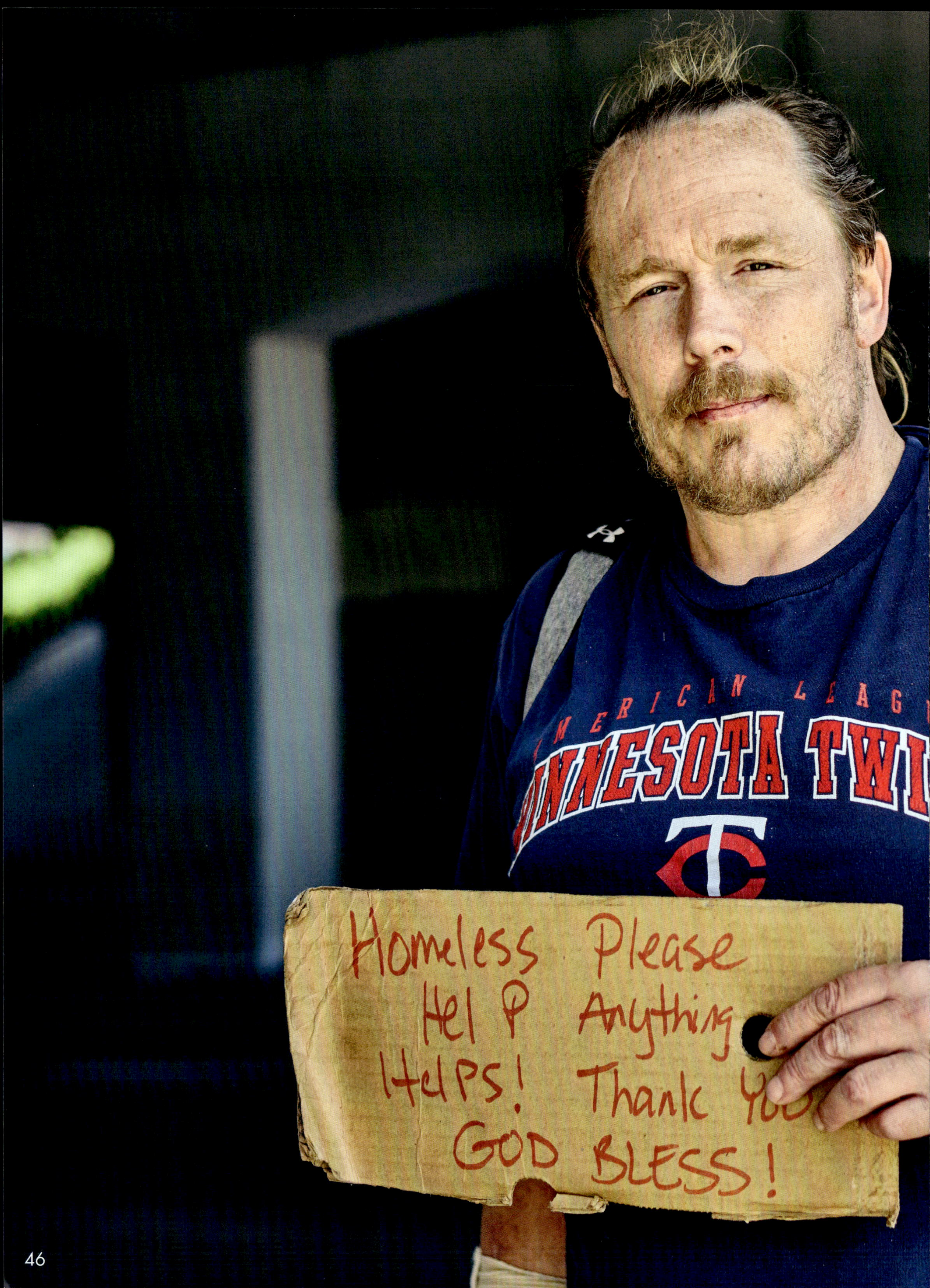
Homeless Please
HelP Anything
HelPs! Thank Yo
GOD BLESS!

Charles W.

Every New Year, many people make a resolution to change. This change isn't the kind found lingering forgotten in our pockets, copper-coated remnants carelessly tossed to pitiful beggars. No, once meaningful, that kind of change now seemingly holds little value. True change – the life-altering kind – is not measured by its monetary value but in the currency of commitment. Taking action is the first step. Moving from aspiration to perspiration. Of course, it's easier said than done. Charles, or Chuck as he prefers, is keenly aware of this as he stands at an important crossroads. He needs a new direction. Thankfully, he seems willing to take the next vital step toward meaningful change.

Seeking shelter from the sun, we retreat to a shady spot under an overpass near 55 West and Cedar Avenue. Chuck is sporting a blue Minnesota Twins baseball jersey and a thick medical wrapping around his wrist. He candidly shares about the many poor choices he's made in life and how he is beginning to turn some things around.

When he was young, Chuck dreamed of becoming a paid musician. Although he may never fully realize his dream, he still possesses the skills to pursue that goal. "Yeah, I play drums, guitar, and I'm a vocalist...I listen to everything, but I got a David Ruffin sound."

"...just be kind to people. I think that's the biggest thing. Just be kind."

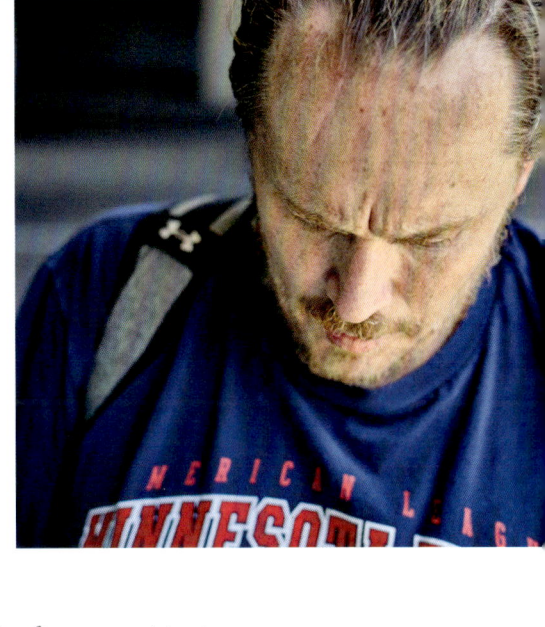

Chuck came to Minnesota from Chicago about nine years ago, hoping for a fresh start. "I came here for a change. I lost everything and, got down on my luck, started using drugs. I wanted to get away from Chicago, so I came here for a change."

Loss has been a theme in Chuck's life. The devastating loss of his mother, who was tragically murdered by his stepfather, hastened his move to Minneapolis. Soon after arriving here, he also lost his biological father. Despite having ample reasons to feel sorry for himself, Chuck hides behind none of this. "Yeah, it was tough, you know. But at the same time, I'm one of those people that believe that you have choices in life. Everybody has something happen to them."

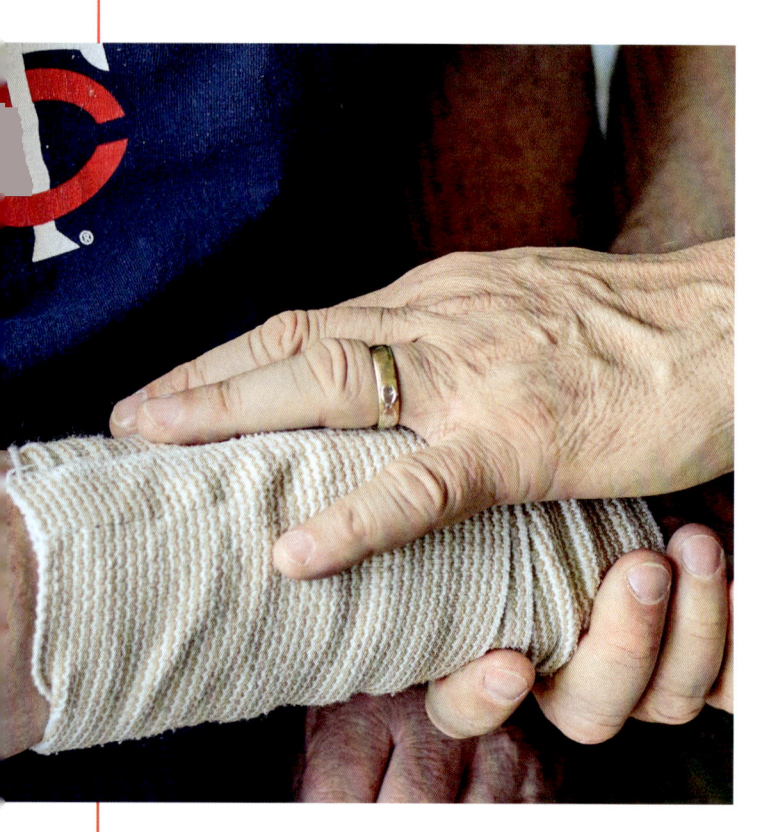

Poor choices, pain, and misery aren't all that Chuck left in Chicago. "I'm divorced, and I have a 25-year-old daughter. She's in Chicago. I don't get to see her much. I talk to her as much as I can."

Moving to Minnesota didn't bring the immediate change Chuck had hoped for. "The guy that brought me here, he actually ended up robbing me for everything I had. I didn't know anybody here at all. I was a heroin addict when I got here. I had to immediately figure out what I was going to do to get some money. It's like everybody else that has to deal with addiction. You find a way to eat and take care of your addiction. I don't like jail, so I chose not to break the law too much."

The thick medical wrapping around Chuck's wrist encases an injury with a story as inspiring as it is harrowing – a hopeful example of something good coming from bad. "So, heroin and meth. Tough stuff to deal with. I used to mix the shots together. I've been an intravenous drug user for about 20 years. And after a while, my body started rejecting it, and my arm got infected. It's happened before, and the hospital did a bedside procedure instead of a surgery. It was so painful that I was scared to ever go back to the hospital. So, I waited too long and almost lost my arm. I had to do some soul-searching while I was in the hospital. I said that if I could get out with my arm (not being amputated), I would change my ways. And so, that's what I've done. I'm going to treatment next week. You know, it's time for a change."

"You know, it's time for a change."

With aspirations fueled by his experiences on the Minneapolis streets, Chuck envisions leveraging this newfound perspective to help others in need. But he also knows that before he can help others, he must first commit to his own personal growth. "I really want to make a change for myself first," he asserts.

> " I'm one of those people that believe that you have choices in life. Everybody has something happen to them."

As we close our time with Chuck, we ask him how someone can help if they have no cash to offer and are simply passing by during a momentary encounter. He shares that simple gifts can go a long way to make things easier for someone experiencing homelessness. "I would say anything that has to do with socks, hygiene, and just food. The other thing is just be kind to people. I think that's the biggest thing. Just be kind."

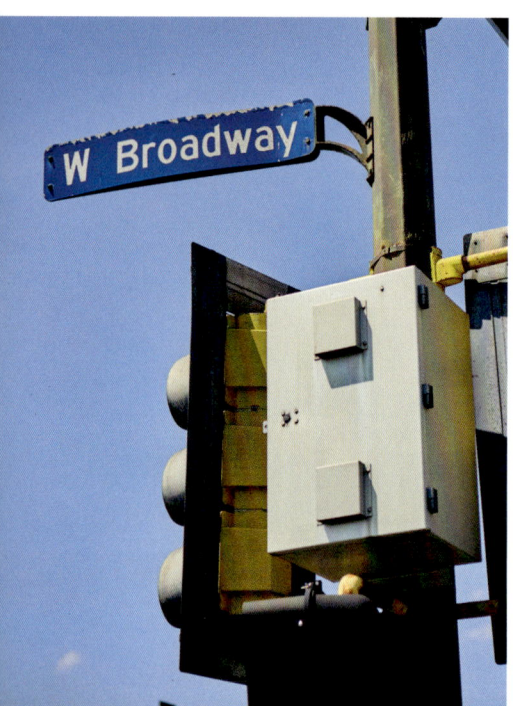

Daisy B.

Meeting Daisy is like encountering a human tsunami of strong opinion and unrelenting resolve. The phrase "Street Smarts" is perfectly embodied in this physically fit, middle-aged mother of four children. She parades tattoos on her arms with biceps that can rightly be called "guns" and sports a decorative ring in her nose. She is funny, intelligent, personable, and swears like a sailor. Whether one agrees with her or not, she presents a strong case for her point of view and is more than willing to engage with us in some friendly verbal sparring. At first glance, one can only wonder how Daisy landed in this place. Her story is unique, yet, in many ways, it is the familiar storyline of so many who end up living on the streets.

> "...are you really homeless? No, I'm just standing here holding a sign because humiliation is one of my hobbies."

Daisy is quick-witted, a clear thinker, and a meticulous planner. She has fashioned several cleverly phrased signs, including the one she was waving when we met, which reads, "Residentially Challenged Anything Helps." She wraps her reusable signs in clear plastic to prevent damage from the elements. As we begin our visit, she claims to have another one that says, "Domicile Deficient." She shrugs and says, "Nobody seems to get the joke."

51

Daisy didn't grow up on the streets, but her upbringing was certainly no picnic either. This Midwestern girl experienced a childhood that was "very abusive in every sense of the word." Her mother abandoned her when she was only sixteen years old. "So I started college early and graduated high school early. Moved to California when I was like seventeen." Daisy's field of study was Economics and Linguistics. "I wanted to go to Law School. I wanted to be a lawyer. Criminal Law," she added. "But when you're fighting to survive, you know, you don't have the emotional bandwidth to address the other needs, like student loans and all those life skills that most regular people take for granted. You don't necessarily have the cognitive development…Plus, you're dealing with all the emotional trauma."

Following her time at university, Daisy met someone she now calls her children's father. "I was 30 because I wanted to wait until I was ready to have kids with someone with whom I could be a stay-at-home mom. So, I wasn't going to enter the workforce until they were all mostly grown. When that didn't work out, it was like, well, s**t, what do I do? Okay, well, I guess I'll figure out something."

One thing led to another, and eventually, Daisy ended up where she is today: living in a local shelter with four children, struggling to make ends meet, trying to save up enough to get a home, and providing the best sense of normal she can for her family. Daisy confides that it's difficult living like this, and she feels like a bad mother to her children.

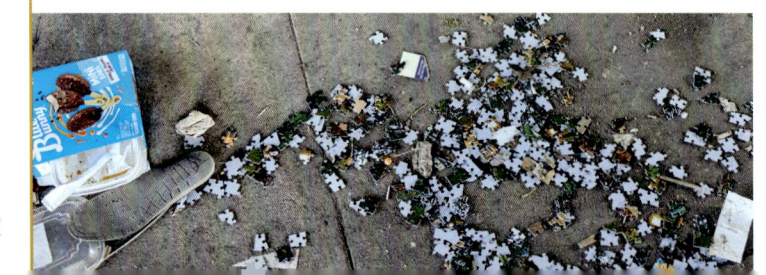

In addition to signing at intersections, Daisy works a full-time job, bartending and waiting tables from 3:00 pm until 1:00 am, and then doing most of her panhandling earlier in the day. It's a long and arduous schedule requiring her children to frequently fend for themselves. At least, she says, "they're old enough to be unsupervised." But it is not the life she, nor her kids, want to live. "They resent that, you know, like, this is the life that they live. They want to do normal things. Go to the swimming pool, play sports, you know, and I can't do those things for them. I don't want them running the streets of Minneapolis. But what do you do with a fourteen-year-old? And so, I task him with keeping an eye on (his) sister. It wasn't the program he signed up for. So, for now, I'm trying to get enough money (so) if they all want to go to the pool or it's Friday night pizza night, we can, you know, do the simple things."

"The people that have the least to give, give the most. The people that have the most to give, give the least. But they're going to have a pretty lonely life in that castle, I'm guessing."

For Daisy and her family, she says living in a shelter is a daily reminder that they "are not part of society. You're just on the outside of it. I don't have a little yard that I can garden. My kids don't have a living room they can sit in, where they can invite their friends over, and feel normal. We stay in Mary's Place, which is a godsend, but a nun comes around every morning at nine o'clock and inspects our house. It's really dehumanizing and degrading. I know why they do it. I've got four kids in three rooms. Like, what do you expect?"

Is this what Daisy dreamed her life would be like – raising four children, working a full-time job, and countless hours on the boulevard entertaining the public like a court jester, just to collect commuters' coins of compassion?

"You know, when I was in second grade and drawing a picture of 'what do you want to be when you grow up?,' It wasn't a bunch of cars and me standing next to a freeway. Provide me an opportunity to feed myself and do for myself, and I'd be much happier." Daisy says most people simply do not understand who she is or what she's about. "They see, they think, they figure either I'm on drugs or I f****d up somehow, and this is, like fun for me. Or, are you really homeless? No, I'm just standing here holding a sign because humiliation is one of my hobbies. And the alternatives are what? Well, I could work in… I could be a sex worker. I'd say ten or twelve times a day, I get solicited for the most foul sex work you'd imagine. So, they assume because I'm standing there asking for money that they better get something for it. You know there's a whole series of other things I could do. And for me, this seemed like the most honest thing that was the most economical. The other f****d up part is that there are some days, not very often, but I make more money standing here doing this than I would at a job."

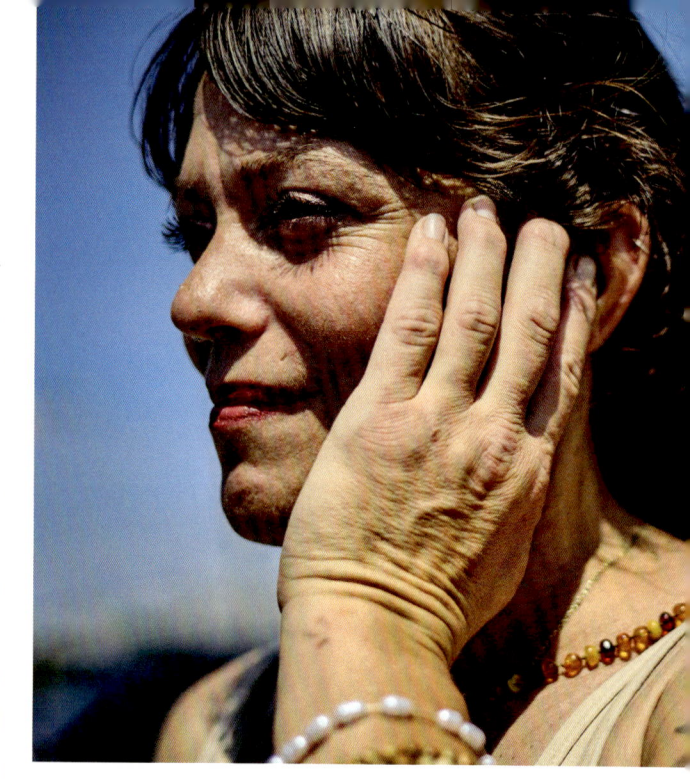

The irony and disappointment of her position weigh heavily on her. Daisy knows that in different circumstances, she might be living a very different life. "Like I'm a college graduate who is probably smarter than ninety-five percent of these a**h***s driving by me. All I want to do is go sit down in the air conditioning, too. I wish I could afford a car and a home, too. I wish that I had that. You know? And the funny part is the people with the most expensive cars are the ones who work the hardest to not make eye contact. The people with the broken windows that have to open their door, they'll give me their loose change. That's always interesting. The people that have the least to give, give the most. The people that have the most to give, give the least. But they're going to have a pretty lonely life in that castle, I'm guessing."

Daisy dreams of finding a permanent, decent place for her family to live. "I'm trying to save as much money as I can and then try to find housing. You know, a modest duplex house in a somewhat decent neighborhood anywhere within the city limits. I just need somebody who may have a little shack, and I'll fix it up. I can lay floors and put in carpet and do all sorts of stuff."

"Provide me an opportunity to feed myself and do for myself, and I'd be much happier."

She grew up in the church, and she has some pointed words to those who want to give to her, and particularly those who hand out religious literature. "Here's the thing if you really want to reach those people, the best way to get them to listen to your message of the gospel is to give them the money so they can do whatever they want with it."

Daisy subscribes to the idea that people won't care what you believe until they believe that you care. "Their ears are open that much more, and that's the little-known secret…The whole society is telling them they're an epic failure and they can't manage their own life. But even if they're going to take that five dollars and go straight to the dope man or straight to the liquor store…they're more likely to hear what you have to say because they feel like you're giving them the respect of personal autonomy. Don't make it your business to run their life."

Daisy would say, if you see her, and you don't want to offer cash or something useful, at least acknowledge her standing there. "Don't ignore me like I'm the scum of the earth and not there." She says sometimes begging on street corners "doesn't necessarily always bring out the best in you. There's a lady that drives by a lot that says, 'Are you going to ever do anything with your life?' and I just want to punch her in the face. Like, are you kidding me? You're fifty pounds overweight!"

Daisy is also not amenable to those who give nothing but religious literature. She has a Christian faith, but admittedly, it's quite raw and rather salty. Still, there's a certain charm in her practical outlook. "I grew up in the church, so I get it. But these people that hand me these fire and brimstone pamphlets…like, I can't hand this to a landlord, bro…Like, just keep it. It's just one more thing that I'm not going to want to carry around. Don't hand me that as if it's going to magically fix it all. Like, if I accept Jesus in my heart, is there suddenly going to be a house over here that I can walk into? And I don't think Jesus would have come up and told me, like, 'Come unto Me.' He'd have been like, 'Yo, b***h, you want five dollars?' He'd have met me where I'm at, you know. Listen, I don't think in the scheme of things that He's really worried about my 's**t' or my F-bomb here and there. And He wouldn't have cared what the five dollars was for or any of that. I'm trying to accomplish a goal, and that's like, put some money together to be able to go to the grocery store."

We closed our time together with a word of prayer that Daisy might someday soon find a home to fulfill her dreams. Admittedly, this woman, some might call off-color, also has a lot of charm, intelligence, and irreverent audacity. She lives by a simple philosophy: "We can make a decision every morning. You can be a total s**thead or put positive energy out into the world." Although she has a fighter's spirit and the physicality to back it up, she prefers to express kindness.

Following our prayer together, we gave Daisy some gift cards to help her buy a few extra things for her family. She was blessed and exclaimed, "You're the s**t. We can get underwear and pizzas!" We asked which comes first, underwear or pizza? She thought about it for a moment and said, "Man, that's a hard choice. You can wash the underwear, but pizzas…you can't."

It was an unforgettable encounter with this even more unforgettable "Residentially Challenged" person. Kudos to Daisy the "Domicile Deficient" supermom!

GOD is LOVE
REJOICE ALWAYS
Jesus Loves You
Give Thanks
JESUS is LORD
KING JESUS
HALLELUJAH
Thanks, Jesus
WALTCO

58

Frederick (Dre) W.

Dre may come across as a tough guy, but he has a gentle heart. This is obvious in the love he shows for his bulldog, Ory, named to remind him of his New Orleans roots. He mentions her well-being before his own. "This is my dog. This is my only family I have here. I need to try to make me some money so I can get my dog some dog food and a few things." Ory is obviously precious to Dre.

Dre isn't shy about admitting his shortcomings. He spoke at length about how a series of poor decisions changed the trajectory of his life, including abandoning his dream of playing football.

"Yeah, I was pretty good. I played defensive end. I played running back. I was versatile. I was just good. I was really good. I thought I was too good to go to practice. I went to practice when I wanted to. But I didn't go to practice like I was supposed to. And that caused me to miss games. And I was getting aggravated. I started drinking. I wasn't doing no drugs, but I was doing a lot of heavy drinking. And so when I did start to play, I started losing my ability. Because I had started drinking. Then I messed up my ACL. So that really took me out. I just messed myself up."

Dre admitted his poor choices derailed his family life, causing the end of his marriage. With a football career no longer an option for Dre, he began associating with some unsavory characters. "So, I had a couple of friends. They was doing their thing.

So I took a chance and I started doing their (illegal) stuff. It took only one time, and I got incarcerated. I did six and a half years. After I came home, I got straight and me and my girl got together. And we had two kids, a son and a daughter. I had a gambling habit at the same time. I gambled a lot of money away. So, we wound up getting a divorce."

From there, things went from bad to worse. A car accident put Dre in his wheelchair. Yet despite the tragic injury and all he's been through, he gives thanks to God for the things that have gone right.

"I want to see a change in life where we love each other. Everybody getting along, and there's no more violence. That's what I would like to see."

"I flipped over eight times. I messed up my back real bad. They said if I would have flipped over one more time, I would have broke my back. So, God is good. I know God is good. He saved me. Because I was in some people's backyard. I hit the back of their house. They thought a tree fell. My body hit the house. But the house was wood. If it would have been concrete, I probably would have died. Because that's how hard I hit the house."

Dre lived in the 9th Ward in New Orleans at the time of his accident. The city was hit hard by Hurricane Katrina in 2005, and the damage to key infrastructure, such as hospitals, was a problem when Dre needed critical medical care. "Because of Katrina. They didn't have neurosurgeons. They had a lot of interns. So they couldn't do no surgery. My back was getting real, real bad. I couldn't even walk. So people had to pick me up and put me in a car to bring me to this and that."

Dre ended up in Minnesota because his sister's friend suggested that he come here for medical treatment. It was another decision that would change the trajectory of his life. Dre is finally getting the treatment he needs to get back on his feet, figuratively and literally.

"Minnesota is amazing. They did an operation on my back. It took 11 hours and 26 minutes. I will never forget this doctor. His name was Dr. Thomas Bergman. That was my doctor. And now I'm about to have a hip specialist setting it back. They say they want the antibiotics to work because if the antibodies don't work and they do the hip surgery on me, it can cause me to get my leg amputated."

Speaking about his experiences as he is holding a cardboard sign on the street corner, Dre shares that he has chosen a new path for his life. Despite the emotional toll it takes, he would rather beg than rob or steal. But he misses being self-sufficient. "Oh, man, it's humiliating. It's degrading. But I do what I got to do. I'm not going to go steal or rob nothing. I don't never want to go back to prison."

Dre is working on putting his life back together, but it's a slow process – a process our support systems can sometimes complicate. By taking available benefits, he risks forfeiting some future benefits that could make the difference between couch surfing or getting his own place. "I'm waiting to get my place. It's a process, but I got a friend that I'm staying with now. My sister's sending me money until I'm able to get myself on my feet."

Dre has endured a lot of things, but his worst moment on the street was when someone choked him, and Dre was barely able to defend himself due to his physical limitations at the time. It was a painful experience, but Dre chose to see that moment as a lesson in forgiveness, offering further proof that he has chosen a new direction for his life, free from anger and resentment.

"See, you can't always just ask God to forgive a person, but you got to see what you did to cause that. And God will put something on your mind like, 'Do you remember that time 10 years ago? Remember what you did?' You know what I'm saying? So, it fades away just like a sore or something. If you don't pick the scab, it'll heal. So, I just left it alone, and it healed. Now, if I see him again, I can just look at him and do that (forgive) because the strength didn't come from me. So, I can do that now."

When asked what he wants for the future, Dre prioritizes the greater good over his own needs. His response reflects a heart that has been changed and truly cares for others.

I want to see a change in life where we love each other. Everybody getting along, and there's no more violence. That's what I would like to see."

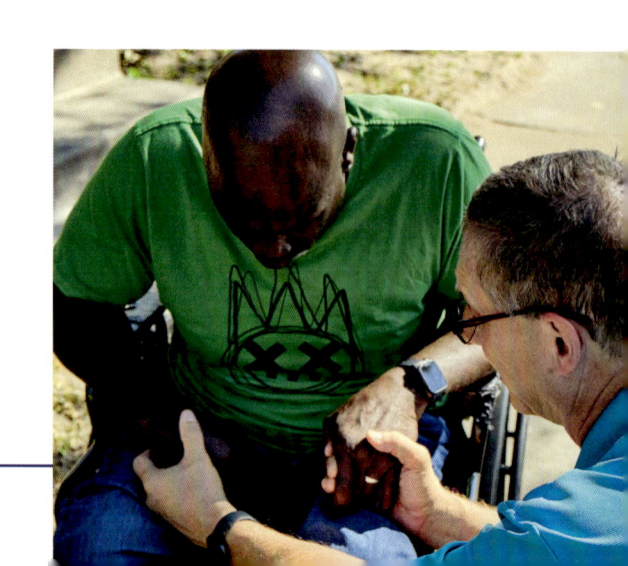

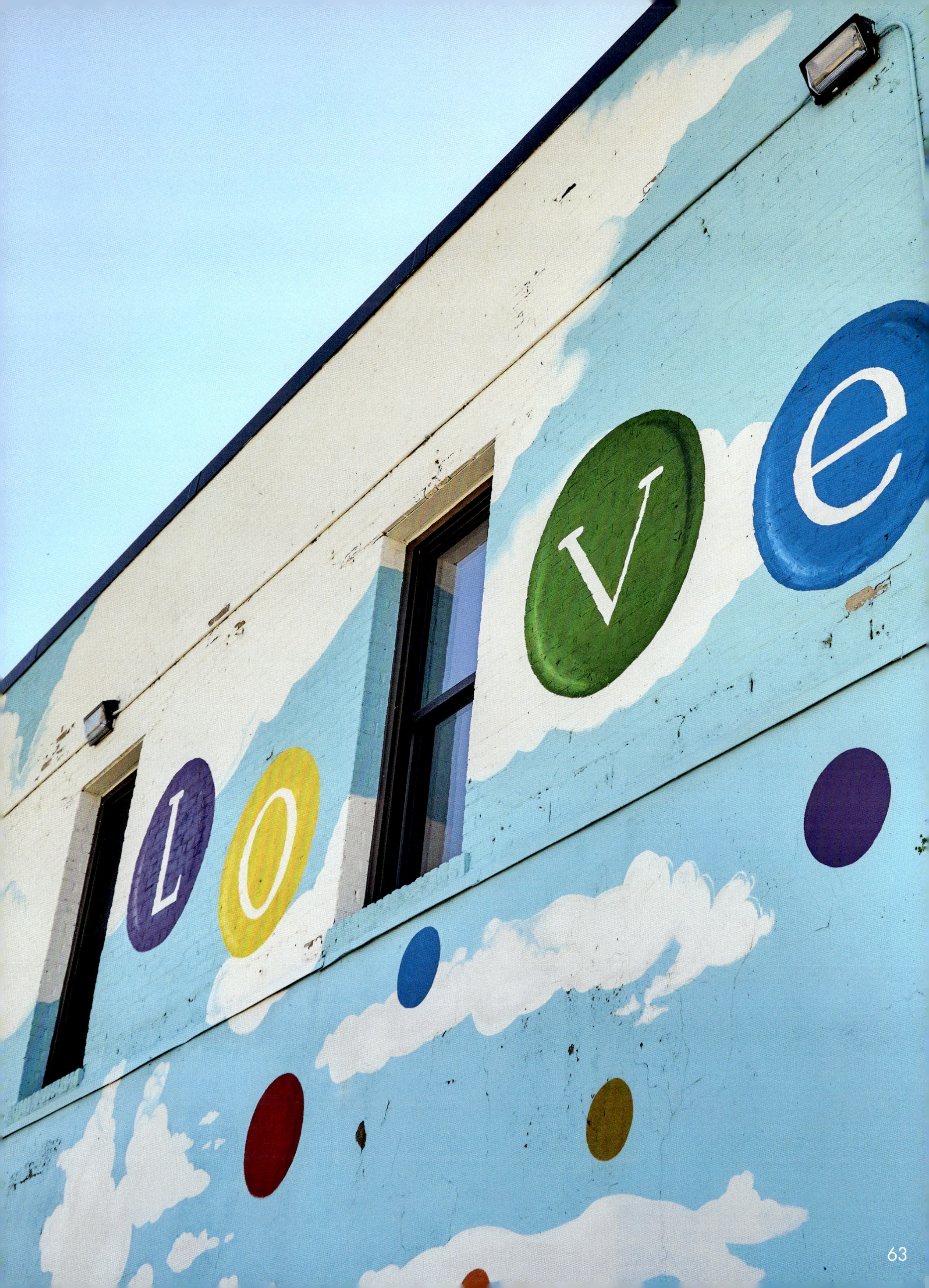
LoVe

Jade F.

Meeting someone under an inner-city bridge in a rough area of town is usually considered a recipe for trouble. One can only wonder about the many sordid deals, unsavory exchanges, and sleazy activities that may have happened in this cavernous underpass. It's a real life bridge over troubled waters and the regular hangout and the temporary home of several unhoused humans.

Despite our surroundings – the graffiti-stained cement walls and a slew of discarded needles, unwanted debris, and abandoned shopping carts – we somehow have a meaningful connection with a soft-spoken and gentle soul named Jade. He's not the sort of person one assumes would successfully survive in this less-than-palatial urban courtyard.

Jade blends in easily and can almost go unnoticed. He is slightly taller than the average person and, on this cool April morning, is sporting somewhat disheveled hair. He has a welcoming face, deeply penetrating coal-colored eyes, and a natural caramel complexion. His teeth are worn and appear to be in very poor condition. Jade rarely allows his teeth to show, even when his face lights up in a good-natured smile. His hands are rough, beaten, and stained with dirt and grime, stark evidence of living life on the streets. As we converse with Jade, he seems a tad wistful, with a hint of regret, as he reflects upon his life.

"I think I'd like to be seen as, you know, like not less than them."

One might expect to hear a self-pitying sob story; however, Jade surprisingly challenged our assumptions by proudly announcing, "I try to stay happy all day." He exudes a certain positivity that feels out of place amid the remnants of this South Minneapolis tent community.

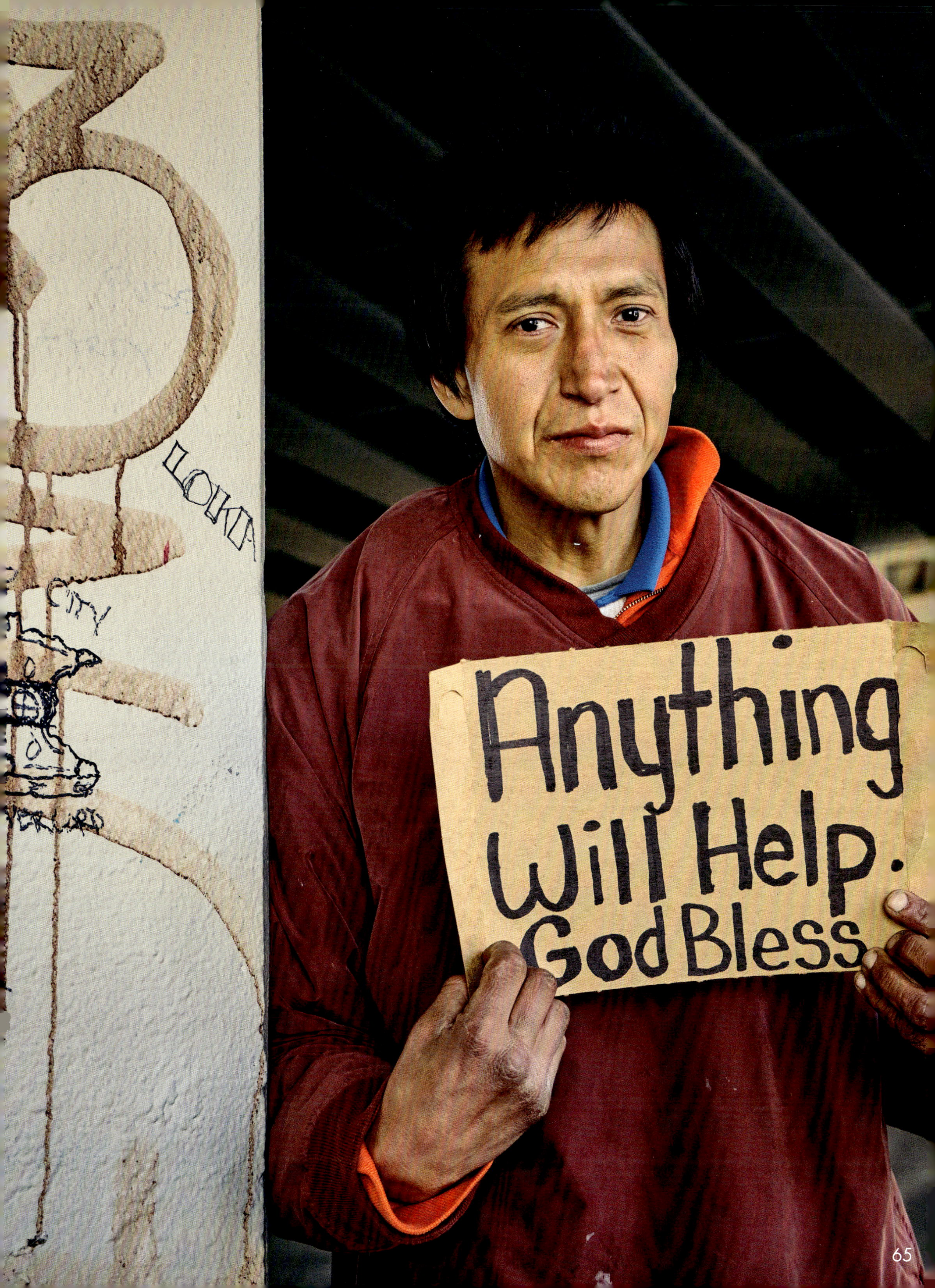
Anything
Will Help.
God Bless

Jade shares his story with us, but the noise of the city regularly drowns out his soft voice – light rail announcements, the clattering sounds of passing traffic on a busy overhead highway, a squad car bullhorn demanding the loitering masses move on… to wherever moving on might be. For these unwanted people, this miserable underpass serves as their porch, their park, and their playground.

In 1994, this same neighborhood was found to have arsenic-based pesticide contamination in its soil and groundwater. Ironically, it symbolizes how the residents and the community have sometimes felt mistreated. It's a place where urban blight and concerns for human rights are often relocated rather than remedied.

Jade has not always lived here. He was born in Yankton, South Dakota, the youngest of seven brothers. "I got picked on…A LOT." Jade shared that he experienced "a lot of hard times" during his younger years. His family moved to Minnesota, where he had no positive support. As a child, Jade had hopes and genuine aspirations for a meaningful future. "I was really ambitious for graphic design, or to become a construction tech." He mused that perhaps one day he'd like to become "a supporting husband." Unfortunately, none of this has worked out for Jade. Unable to finish high school, he told us, "I got my GED in the penitentiary. I worked jobs and stuff. I went to school for automotive." Unfortunately, he had to drop out before he could finish the program.

Jade continues to have aspirational interests, but has no concrete goals. He does not have a good mentor to guide him toward a meaningful path forward or to challenge his undisciplined lifestyle. Jade has become an aimless wanderer, mostly living outside in a tent or using shelters during the winter months. Jade has found the fastest way to earn a few dollars for food and personal items is to stand on the corner waving his sign. It brings in just enough money for him to get by.

"Stay positive and keep a smile on. That's what I do."

At this point in his life, Jade has one primary objective. "I just want to make it through the day." Besieged by a daily battle with depression and relentless despairing thoughts, Jade does his best to smile himself out of this haunting sense of hopelessness. "I try to stay happy all day." It's the very same advice he would give anyone facing similar challenges. "Stay positive and keep a smile on. That's what I do."

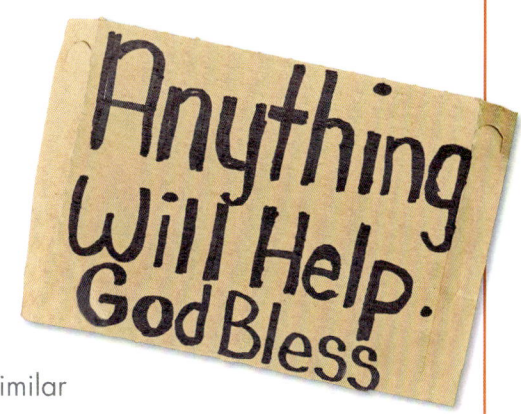

His sign may say, "Anything will help," but for Jade, money is what makes him feel most secure and enables him to survive at least one more day. As we concluded our interview, Jade shared what is ultimately the most meaningful gesture to him. "I'm viewed as being 'less than' them (the commuting public). I think I'd like to be seen as, you know, not less than them." Jade simply wants to be seen as a human being, as a person rather than a bother or a burden.

Isn't this the same dignity and significance we all long for?

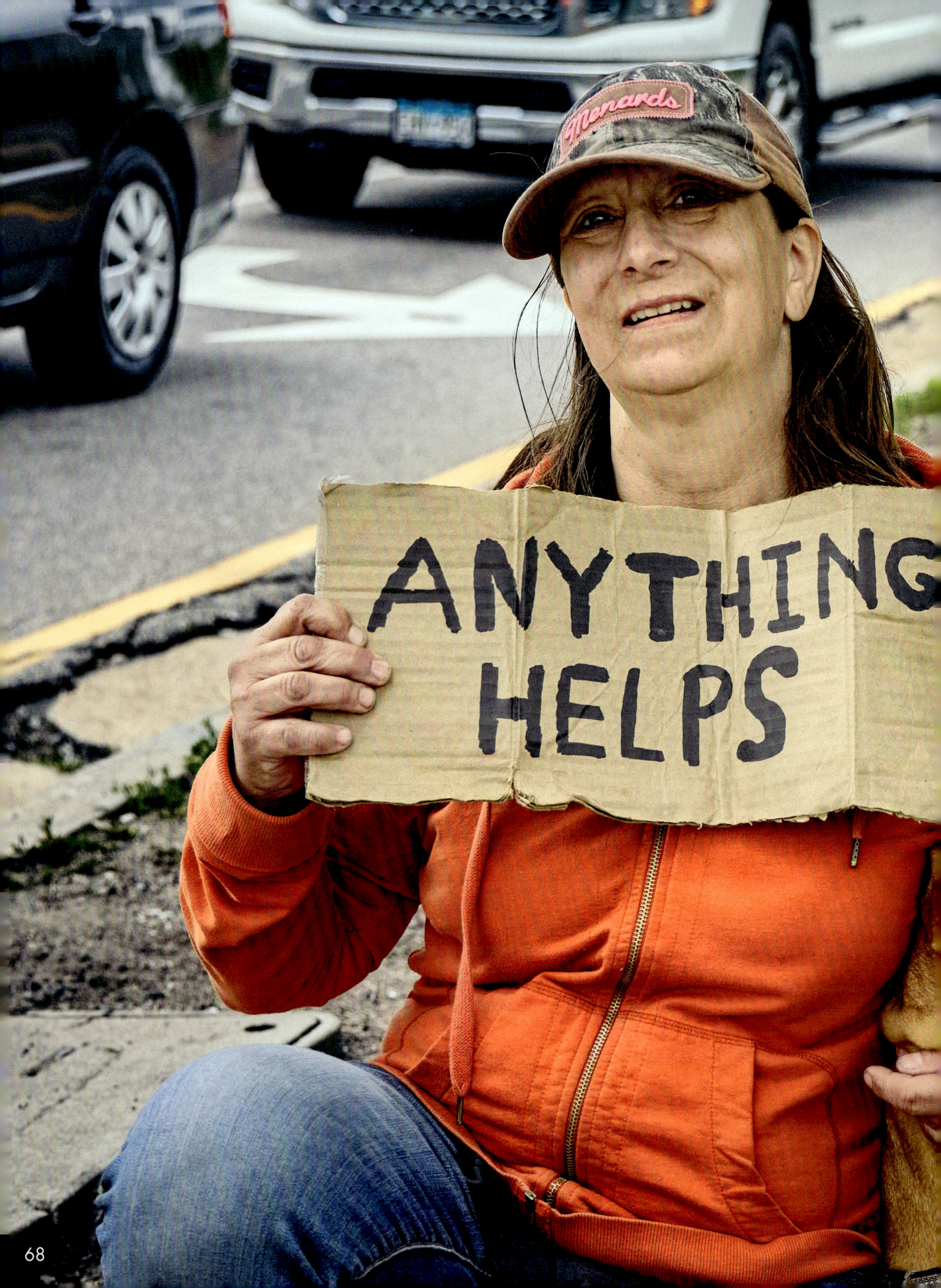
Menards
ANYTHING
HELPS

Jennifer S.

Jennifer, or Jen as she prefers, has a certain earthy ruggedness about her. Wearing denim jeans, an orange zippered hoodie, and a Menards baseball cap pulled low over her eyes, Jen is dressed as if she's heading off to a blue-collar job, like someone who is ready to swing a hammer. Even her weathered hands seem to fit the part.

We meet with Jen on a busy corner near downtown St. Paul, accompanied only by her reddish-brown short-haired dog, Dukoda. Her sign is dressed as plainly as she is. It simply reads, "ANYTHING HELPS." Jen is a get-to-the-point kind of person. Initially wary, she quickly warms up to us. Her tough demeanor belies a naturally kind and personable disposition.

Jen is smart, savvy, and somewhat of a free spirit. She prefers to run her own schedule and doesn't like being tied down by day-to-day responsibilities. Jen seems to carry herself like a hard-working citizen. Yet, ironically, she isn't working… at least not a job that offers a taxable wage. "I got two degrees. Medical lab tech and I don't like doing that. I hated it. And then, I have a two-year preschool teaching degree. I did daycare at my home. I was a nanny for a while. I've done a lot of different jobs. House cleaning. I was a legal aide. My daughter was a lawyer for a while, so I was a legal aide."

"…because I know this area. I feel safer here. I know where to go."

For Jen, it was drug addiction that turned her stability on its head and brought her much pain and loss. "I'm five months sober off meth. I had some real bad problems for a while. I had a house for 20 years in Arden Hills. Lost that because my husband got addicted to meth, and then I got on it. And we lost the house. I was homeless probably four or five times from 2016 until three years ago. And then my mom died, and I inherited $118,000. I bought a house in Wisconsin for $26,000 cash, and it's only $500 a year in property taxes, so I figure I'll never be homeless again…hopefully."

To avoid losing her current home, Jen panhandles to generate income and pay her bills. "I'm doing this now because I ran out of the inheritance after three years, and this is how I made money before. I started doing it and learning I could make money. So now that's what I'm doing, so I can take care of my house up there. First time I did it, I'm going to be honest: I made $189 for an hour and 45 minutes. So that's why (I do it). Fridays are the best days. Weekends suck. I'll take those off. It's not worth it. You've got to have the right corner. You've got to stay out here. I've been down here for about a week and a half. I've been averaging $25 to $35 an hour."

Jen lives nearly four hours away and makes regular excursions to the Twin Cities metro area. She says she prefers the Twin Cities "because I know this area. I feel safer here. I know where to go. And I do have a few people around. If I need to shower, there's a truck stop in West St. Paul, too."

"I'll never be homeless again…hopefully."

Sometimes, Jen will stay locally for as long as three weeks or until she can make enough money to last a while, particularly now that her inheritance is gone. "I had to remodel the house. The house was only $26,000, but I had to redo the whole bathroom and kitchen. And so, you know, the money lasted me three years living on it and getting the house and fixing it."

Jen wrongly assumed that having the house would help to restore her broken marriage. "I got back together with my husband when we moved up there. So, he was supposed to get his disability (benefits). And he didn't go through with that. He got back on the drugs. Now, he's in jail. And we're done."

For Jen, her priorities have become more focused and crystal clear: make enough money to never again be homeless, AND to never go back to using drugs. "You know, it's hard. But the last time I quit, it was forced on me. Not through the courts but through my family. And this time it was my choice, so it's going a lot easier. In fact, I've even been around an old friend that does it (meth). And I didn't use. And it made me really proud of myself. I mean, sometimes you can kind of be forced into it (quitting) in the beginning. But if you don't switch over and make that choice that you really want to stay sober, you're not going to. I don't want to lose my house now. I'm starting to build stuff back, and I don't want to lose it. And coming down here and using (drugs) is just going to be counterproductive to what I'm trying to do."

As we consider Jen's story, we may wonder why an able-bodied, educated person is choosing to panhandle for a living. Still, we can appreciate the effort Jen has made to establish a place she can call home and sustain her hard-earned sobriety. While she certainly has not achieved perfection, it's refreshing to know she is taking progressive steps in the right direction.

Juventino Antonio H.

Just a couple city blocks away from Concordia University, we encounter Juventino Antonio, or Antonio as he prefers, wearing a blue jacket and carrying a backpack. If he wasn't holding a cardboard sign, he could easily be mistaken for a student from campus. As a 19-year-old, he should be going to university, concerned about classwork and making friends. Instead, he has been reduced to waving a sign to survive.

Traffic is heavy and rushes by only a few feet from the sandy corner where Antonio has planted himself to be seen by the late-morning commuters. There's a flower garden just across the street. Allianz Field is visible in the distance. The barrenness and poverty of this corner are a stark contrast to the beauty and wealth nearby. It's cold, windy, and overcast.

"Getting my ID. I'm currently looking into a school so I can get my GED."

Born and raised in Saint Paul, Antonio's childhood was not easy. His mother and father weren't married but were together off and on. He also has a brother and a sister. "It was a rough childhood because of a lot of drugs, a lot of violence, and being around that."

Antonio is no stranger to the experience of living on the streets. "I mean, my dad was homeless, so when I was a kid, I got to see his life. He started to become homeless (when) I was... I think, eight or nine, when that stuff happened, and my mom kind of gave us to my grandma to care for us."

Snelling Ave
HOMELESS AND STRUGGLING
NEED HELP ANYTHING WELL
HELP GOD BLESS
YOU!!

Tragically, Antonio lost his mother in 2022, at the tender age of 16. "It was an abusive relationship with another man. We had two court dates, and they didn't really do nothing. And then he just kind of flipped the scene and just left Minnesota altogether. It turns out that he did this to two other females in two different states."

The loss hit Antonio very hard. To soothe the emotional pain, he struggled with Fentanyl use for a couple of years, but he's overcome that habit now. "I mean, you know, growing up without a mother. Not having a mom to see you grow up into your adulthood is really tragic and traumatizing because you would want her to see all this stuff that you're doing, but she can't. It's upsetting."

Antonio struggles to maintain a healthy and consistent relationship with his family. "I don't really have anywhere to go. I mean, my family members are all spread out. Most of my family don't want to talk to anyone right now because of my mom… it's hard."

Reflecting on his former struggles with drugs, Antonio seems determined not to fall into that pattern again. He avoids asking for help from folks he knows might bring those troubles back into his life. He wants to respect the kind intentions of those caring souls who offer him a few dollars. "Some of these people that are out here don't really use the money for food. They use it just to get high, and it's just like… I can't do that. It's disrespectful, and it's how could you go on living your life saying that you're homeless and then not try to fix it?"

Antonio lives on the streets with only a few meager belongings and a sleeping bag. He sees a friend daily who helps him by caring for his belongings. Thieves have robbed Antonio a few times, causing him to lose his birth certificate and driver's license, including when he has taken shelter on the light rail train. Like many in similar situations, Antonio uses public transportation to get out of the elements for a little while. "Literally, no tent, no shelter, just a sleeping bag, just trying to find a safe place. I've had a couple people rob me before, not as I was sleeping, but as I was awake, like, on the (light rail train). That's a real bad place. People get robbed a lot, and a lot of people just don't do nothing to help you. They just watch it happen. It's bad."

So, how did Antonio end up on the streets like his father? The new management evicted Antonio, his siblings, and his grandmother from the apartment where they were staying. Because of this disruption, he was unable to finish high school. Without a high school diploma, finding work is a struggle.

""I don't really have anywhere to go. I mean, my family members are all spread out."

Antonio snickers when asked what he wanted to be when he was younger. "All the teachers asked me that, and I always gave them the same response. Like, I haven't finished high school yet, so why ask me now? I did have, like, a future in mind. I just wanted to have at least a small apartment and at least someone to call my own. Just to have a life, just like… how everyone else does."

Those dreams seem nearly unachievable now, but Antonio has some plans to pull his life back together. The first step, he says, is "Getting my ID. (Then) I'm currently looking into a school so I can get my GED, and they've been really helpful too."

Antonio has tried multiple times to access programs that are available to unhoused folks in the Twin Cities, but there are difficulties. Without an ID, it's nearly impossible for Antonio to access the support programs that require identification. Then, there are gaps in the timing and availability of food resources. "There's like those food trucks that come around for the homeless, and I go there. I try to catch one at least every day, and I go to churches and stuff like that, but it's every other week, and it's like 'We only do Thursdays until 11:00 a.m.,' and by the time I'm there everyone's already eating everything and, you know, it's like 'Oh we have apples and crackers.'"

Similar to many we have spoken to, Antonio doesn't expect much from others, other than basic respect and human kindness. "I see a couple people when I'm signing that come back around and talk. Come to visit me on a daily basis, and if they have money, they'll give me like a couple dollars and stuff. But usually, they just come and talk and give me some snacks and stuff. It makes me feel like they care."

Amid his nomadic lifestyle on the streets, Antonio seems to appreciate those who take the time to reach out to him. Like most of us, he wants to feel that he is valued and has significance. For Antonio, in part, this means restoring his inner identity, which involves far more than merely securing a new government ID card. It's about human dignity and being respected by others in a spirit of genuine kindness and care.

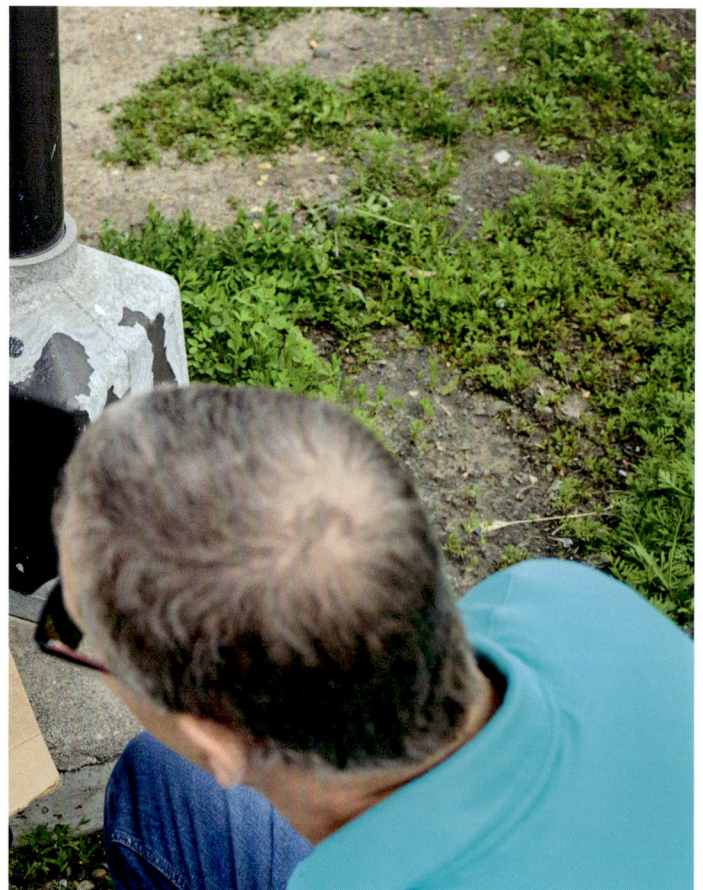

77

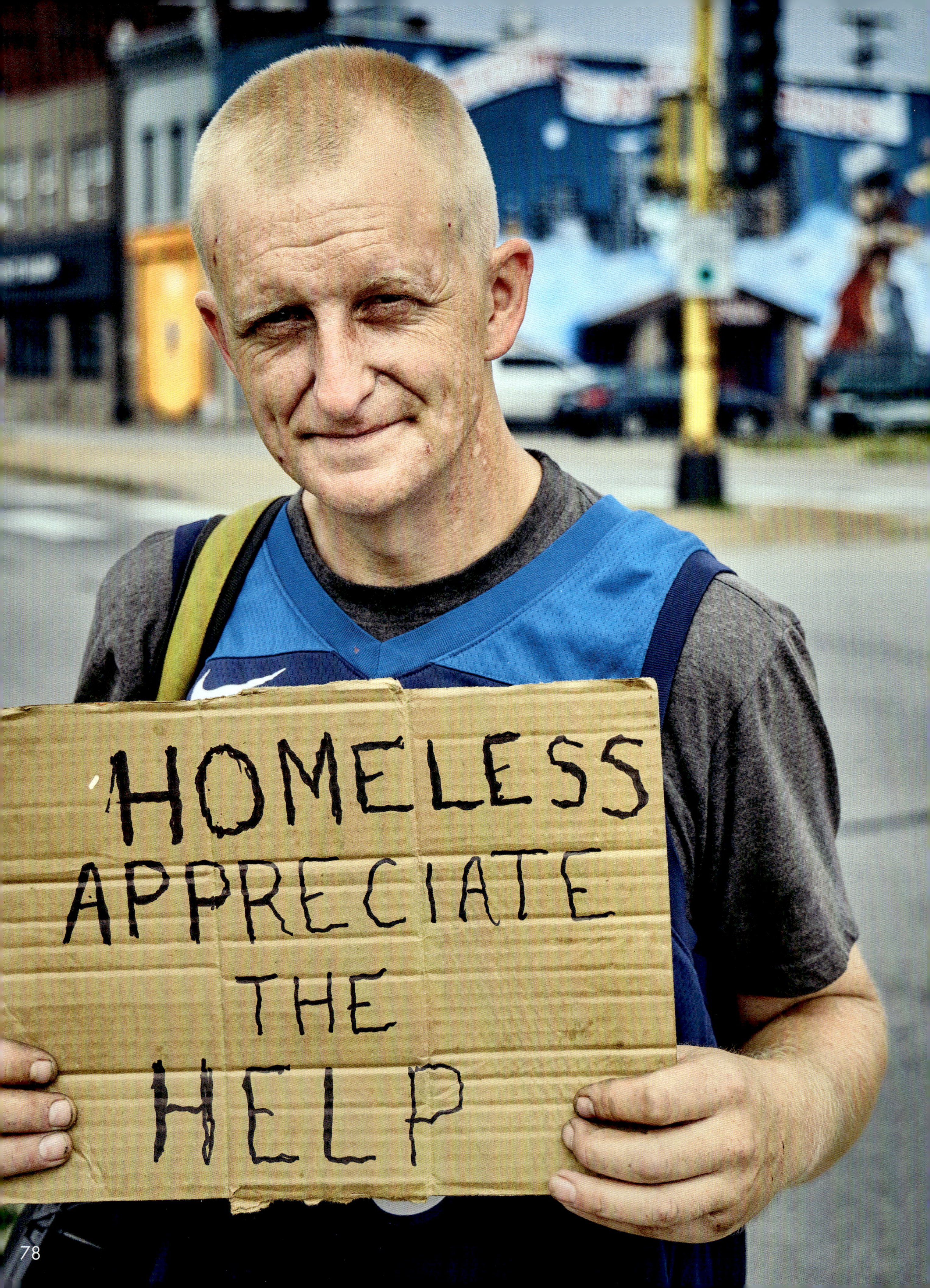
HOMELESS
APPRECIATE
THE
HELP

Keith A.

At some point in our lives, most of us have experienced "bone-tired weariness." Not the ordinary tiredness we typically shoulder, but the kind of exhaustion that feels overwhelming, saturating, and presses deep into the fissures of our body and soul. A type of fatigue that causes our entire being to droop… barely able to lift, or even drag our heavy feet forward. There is no remaining motivational reserve, no vim, or vigor. Not even the energy to express emotion, or to think another rational thought, much less to care for the very basics of life. It's as if even the clothing we wear mirrors our exhaustion, clinging to our body like a long-oversized trench coat haplessly slung on a hanger. This is "bone-tired weariness."

For people on the streets, like Keith, this is all too often their normal state of existence. Striving to maintain a fraction of hope and a sliver of motivation, just grinding away. In the winter, struggling to stay warm and fight frostbite. In the summer months, searching for a place to get cool amid the scorching hot and humid days or to keep dry when rainstorms flood their makeshift pop-up shelters. The anxiety of maintaining sobriety or to unceasingly find ways to stay safe from assailants.

"You know, I… I've… I don't know… the streets get really exhausting. It's really exhausting."

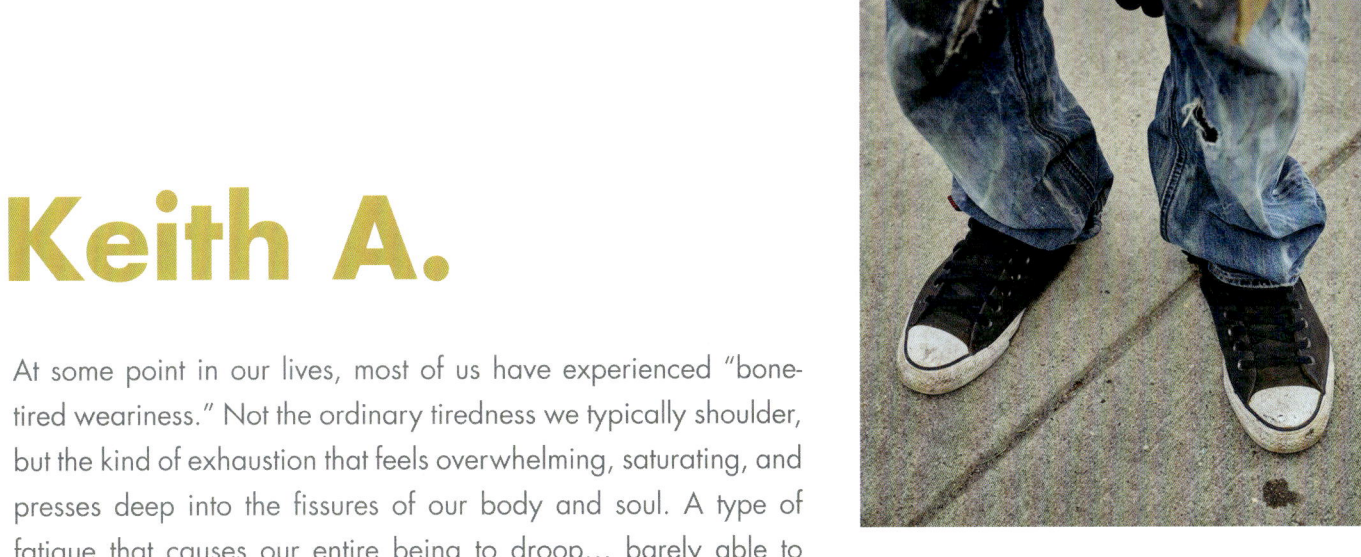

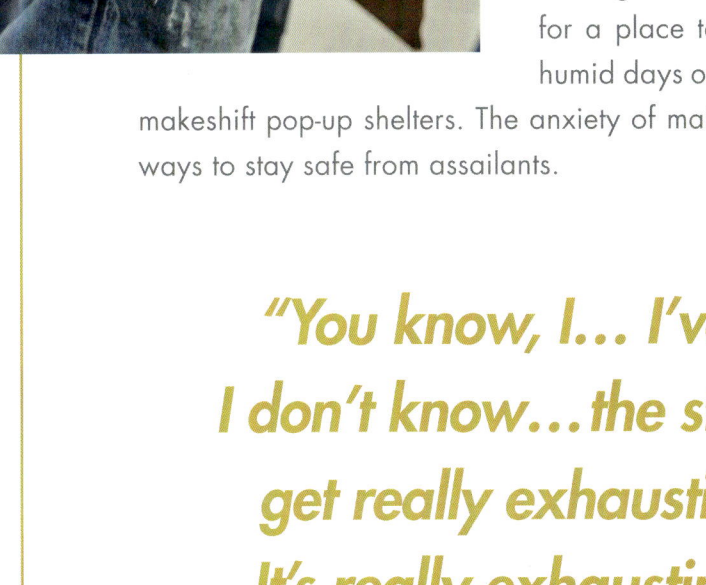

Keith acknowledged the constant stress related to his personal safety. "Yeah, it's always a concern. I can't really lock up the tent, you know? Anyone could just ambush me and take all my stuff anytime. So, it's pretty dangerous. I just move around. I don't stay in one spot too often." He's just struggling to keep his head above the waters in a ceaseless battle to maintain and survive until tomorrow.

Keith's journey into homelessness isn't the pathway you might expect. He didn't fall into it because of poverty, addiction, or some crisis of life. Keith was looking for an experience, or perhaps even a youthful adventure—a desire to break out of the daily grind of society. For Keith, homelessness was neither accidental nor incidental. Strangely enough, it was an intentional choice. "I just kind of reassessed because I was taking everything for granted. I didn't appreciate life, so I just gave all my stuff away. Hit the streets and wanted to start from the bottom and work my way back out. I had a job at the time. The daily grind was just kind of getting to me, you know? Doing everything to pay for, to live, you know? And not get to enjoy any of the money at all. So, you know, that's kind of where I was. I live in a tent right now."

Of course, Keith didn't anticipate how difficult and grueling living on the streets might become. We can all become victims of our own choices when we don't have a community of wise and trusted advisors to help us successfully navigate the best course for our lives. His chosen course the result of a naïve miscalculation, Keith failed to consider how problematic it would be to climb his way back out of his nomadic lifestyle. Keith has grown disenchanted and weary of this life—very weary, bone-tired weary.

"You know, I... I've... I don't know...the streets get really exhausting. It's really exhausting, especially with the summer being mostly rain. It's been pretty f***ing hellacious."

In many ways, Keith falls into a unique category of folks in the sign-waving profession. He grew up having his basic needs met. But despite having that essential stability, Keith always felt like an outsider in his home. Like a modern version of Cinderella, Keith saw himself as the unwanted stepchild to his surrogate family. His formative years were far from perfect; always feeling disconnected. It began when he was given up for adoption at the tender age of two. He told us, "I don't know my dad," and shared that he has limited interaction with his biological mom. As for his brothers and sisters, "I don't really consider them siblings, just acquaintances."

As we probed a bit more regarding his developmental years, and being raised by a foster family, he remarked, they were "straight-edge people, no substance abuse. I just was like... more of the red-headed stepchild. So, you know, I was the one who did all the chores and stuff." Keith's inner agony at having no sense of belonging is nearly palpable. He is emotionally exhausted, knowing there is no clear end in sight for his struggles, nor any foreseeable future with the comfort and support of a trusted community.

Keith's prospects for a better future indeed seem limited. To move forward and to regain his stability, Keith knows he must re-enter the work force. At this point, he has no actionable plan. Instead, lacking the know-how and basic organizational skills, Keith merely hopes for some kind of regular employment. "I'm thinking about getting into the union somehow. Try and do that before I retire. Try and do that before I get too old. You know, while I'm still somewhat young. Try and get a pension out of it or something. I'm about ready to start rebuilding and getting a place. That's just the first step. Getting a place and getting a job."

These sentiments, sprinkled with the words "somehow" and "try," offer an implied confession that he has no practical roadmap for getting there, much less the energy for the journey.

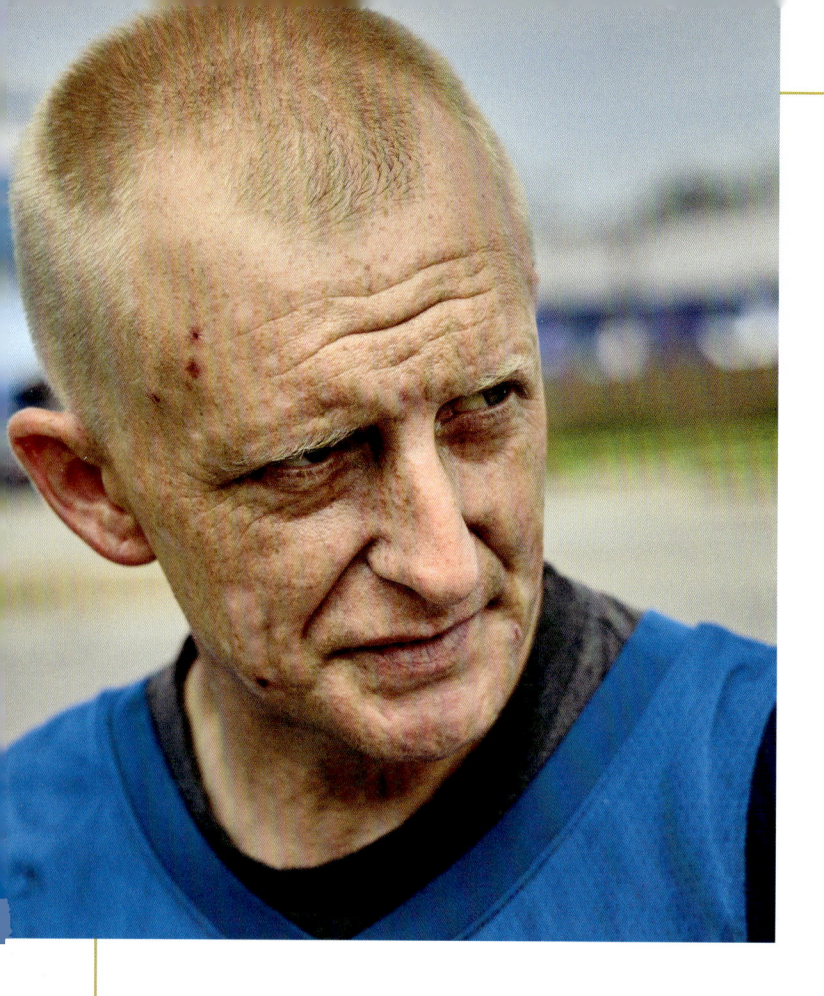

Nonetheless, it seems that deep inside, Keith maintains a small ray of optimism. Despite his personal struggles, he cares about others and longs to be part of a cooperative community. He believes the ultimate gift is being kind. "If someone else doesn't have something…help them out." Keith continued, "The best advice I can give is to help out others when you can. Don't be greedy. You'll find that your help will come back to you."

Keith hasn't always embraced these caring sentiments. "Before, when I had a place to live and I had a job, I would never help out someone that was asking for money. You know, I'd be like, 'Get a job!' The same thing they tell me, you know. Now I understand."

"The best advice I can give is to help out others when you can. Don't be greedy. You'll find that your help will come back to you."

In the meantime, enduring the shame and the pain, Keith continues to beg for money. When asked about his experiences with collecting cash, he blurts, "Negative, very negative." He says he is greeted almost daily with verbal chastisements like, "Get a f***ing job!" Keith just shakes his head with disgust as he remarks, "It gets tiring hearing that s**t." It seems Keith's can-do spirit and his dignity are running on empty, yet with whatever fumes he has left inside, Keith resolutely asserts, "They're not going to take my pride."

Bone-tired of doing time on the streets. Holding to the hope of re-entering what might be considered "regular life." Perpetually looking in from the outside, but never invited to the dance. These concerns have become the footprints of Keith's life.

Our earnest hope and prayer is that somehow, somewhere, this unwanted stepchild will find his perfectly fitted "glass slipper" of opportunity.

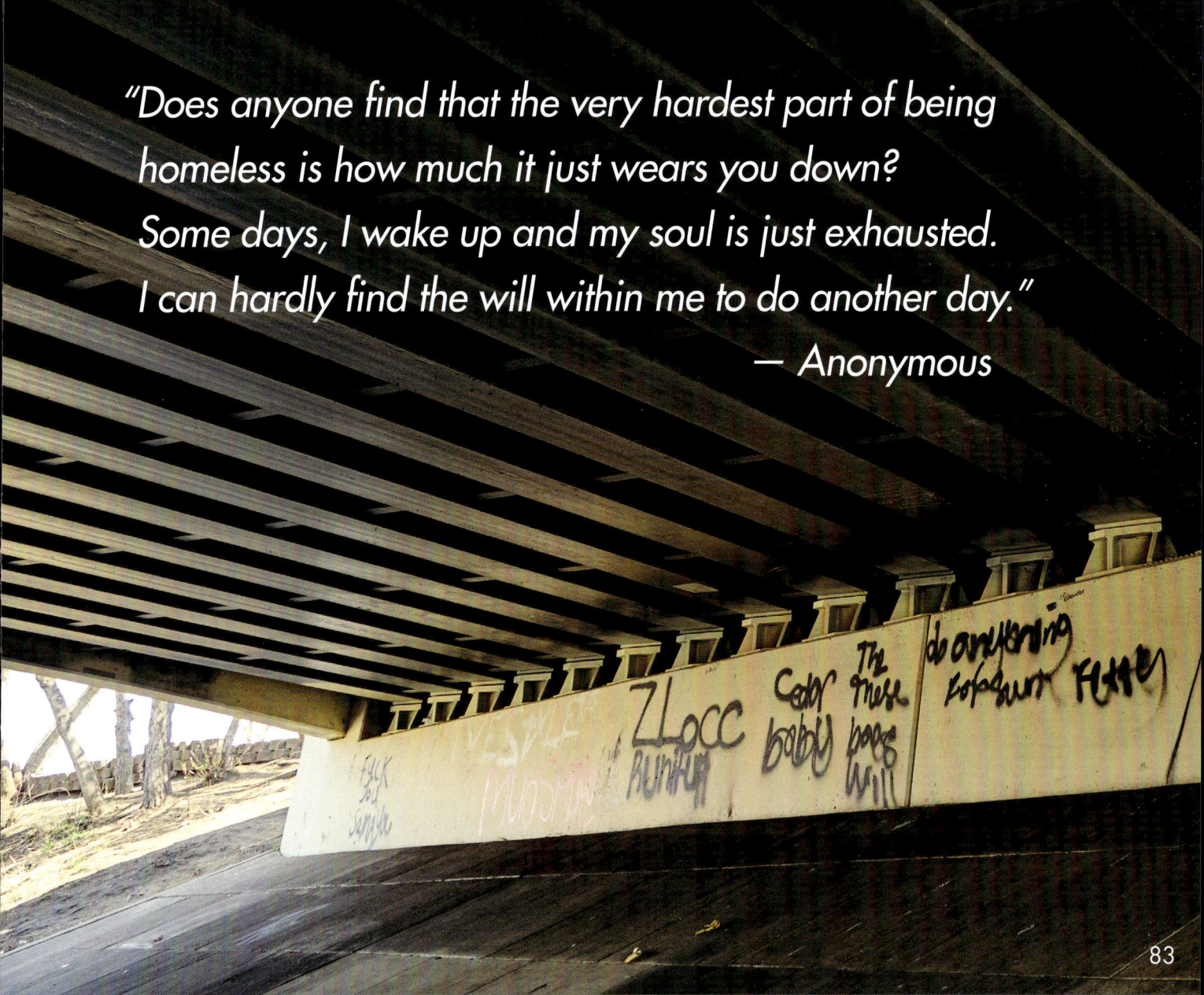

"Does anyone find that the very hardest part of being homeless is how much it just wears you down? Some days, I wake up and my soul is just exhausted. I can hardly find the will within me to do another day."

— Anonymous

Kelsey C.

On this sunny July day, we visit Kelsey, standing on the median at the corner of Broadway and North Washington Avenue in North Minneapolis. With a relaxed expression, Kelsey seems delicate, almost waif-like. She blends in and might go unnoticed if not for her oversized, bright, coral-colored T-shirt. Strangely, on this hot afternoon, she's wearing a blue knitted winter cap and a sweatshirt tied around her waist.

Her sign is barely legible, scrawled in hard-to-read fine-point ink with the simple words, "NEED CASH." Seemingly frail, one can almost picture Kelsey being blown over by an unexpected gust of wind or the turbulent whoosh of a passing semitrailer.

Kelsey's unusually soft manner of speaking perfectly mirrors her slight stature. Her passive voice is nearly lost amid the booming noise of traffic all around us. We imagine Kelsey is a person easily talked over, often overlooked, and sometimes stepped on by others.

Kelsey's pleasant manner makes her seem somewhat vulnerable. One wonders if she is safe in this setting or if someone might take advantage of her. Her calm demeanor reminds us of a delicate flower growing out of place in this harsh concrete cityscape, not typically known for such aesthetics.

For our conversation, we invite Kelsey to move away from the center median of the busy street where she's been waving her sign and into the afternoon shadow of a nearby

"I would like to have my memory back to myself. There's a lot of things that have happened, and I just would like to just sit with myself and have my memory back."

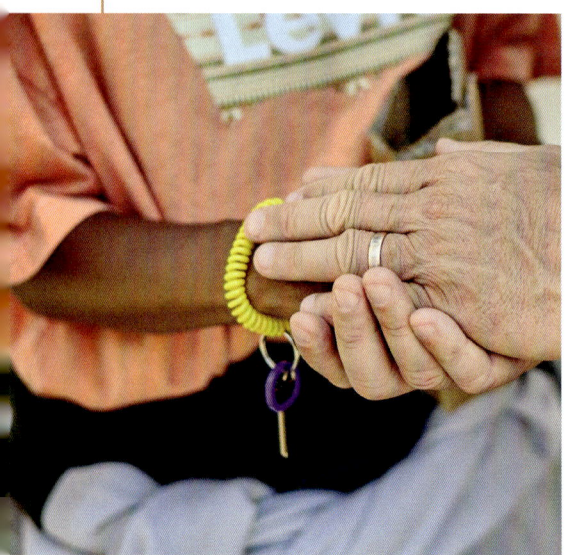

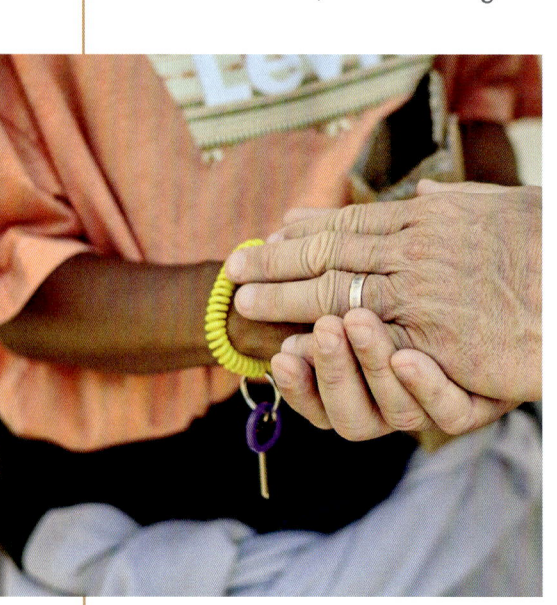

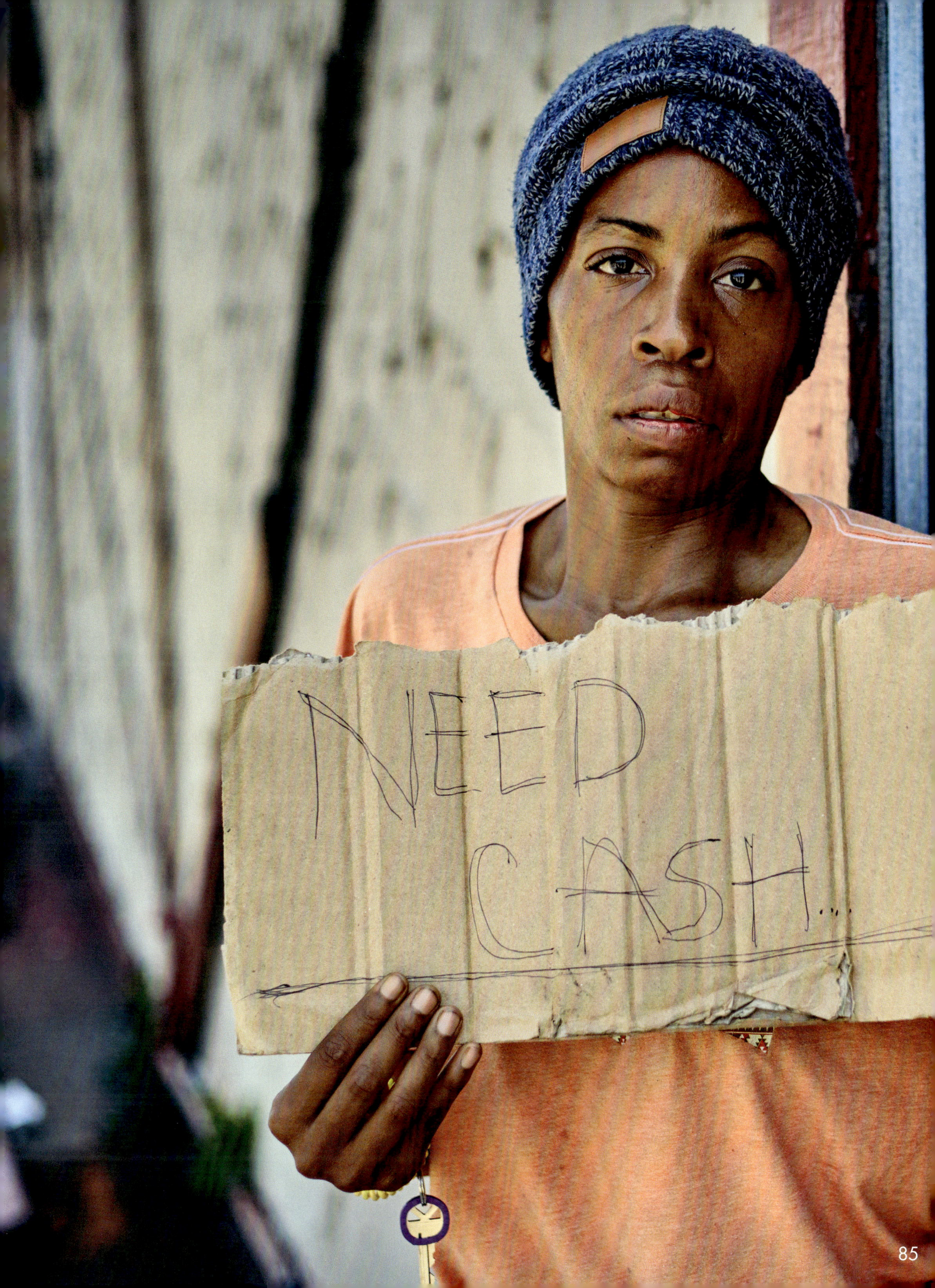
NEED
CASH...

building. It helps to shield us from the directness of the sun, and the shade is a welcome reprieve from the overbearing heat. We begin our conversation by sharing about Good in the 'Hood, our charitable organization. We describe our purpose for visiting with her and the questions we will ask during our interview. We hold the interview microphone close to her mouth to overcome the sound of the large commercial trucks passing by. Their amplified volume reverberates against the brick buildings and concrete sidewalks. Even in a tranquil setting, Kelsey's voice would be barely perceptible. In this loud setting, we strain to hear her words – soft as a whisper, starkly contrasting the blaring city noise all around us.

During our time together, Kelsey shares that she was born locally and grew up in several foster homes. She says these were not good experiences, and she no longer has contact with any of them. However, she stays in touch with her biological parents and siblings. Kelsey does not say why she was in foster homes. Her answers are brief and straightforward, with little elaboration. She isn't particularly guarded; rather, it seems she simply cannot add more information or recall specific details about her past.

We move on, asking Kelsey about the goals and dreams she had as a child. Kelsey tells us she graduated high school, attended North Hennepin Community College, and aspired to become a writer and maybe work in the dental or medical field. "I like to write for a hobby. If anybody finds it interesting, but I don't really like to sell my writing. I just like it to be beautiful and for people to just enjoy it." She then adds, "I'd like to become a dental hygienist and a nurse, and possibly a doctor." We mention that she seems to have a big heart for people, which she affirms is true.

We inquire about her current situation and what has prevented her from completing her education and becoming a dental hygienist. She says, "I just wanted to take some time off, just to be with family."

We asked Kelsey to share some details about her work status. She said, "Well, I just don't like the fact that I would have to stand up and be hurt at work a lot." We're uncertain what kind of 'hurt' she means, emotional or physical. Sharing concerns, possibly about her previous work environment, Kelsey continues, "I would like them to be kind...and that they would understand me and my needs as well. It seems they don't, and whenever I would take a break, I would get written up." Making an educated guess, we asked Kelsey if her feet bothered her. She replied, "Yes, they do." Kelsey continued to explain that even standing for our interview was "kind of painful, a little bit." We mentioned that our charity has a foot care program that is open to anyone, at no cost to our guests. Kelsey expressed interest in this and was grateful for our willingness to help her.

When we asked Kelsey to share about her panhandling experiences, she said, "All I do is hold the sign and get money. They haven't been generous too much, but they're kind." She also said, "They've been helping with food. Just saying 'Hi' helps. Saying God bless me and praying helps. What I'm actually out here for is the cash. Generosity and prayer helps all the time."

> "I would like them to be kind...and that they would understand me and my needs as well."

Kelsey is not homeless. She has a place for now. "I have to come out here and get cash because I don't have regular income coming in right now. I don't have children. I have dogs; I have cats; I have a zoo, actually. Yes, the zoo," she informs us with a smile.

Kelsey's future goals are vague, other than "Just God. God and family, of course. God, family, and friends, and my pets that I have." She says, "There's really nothing holding me back at all."

However, when we ask about her struggles, Kelsey shares something that offers a clue to explain her emotionless and nominal responses. "Some struggles that I have… just with my memory. I would like to have my memory back to myself. There's a lot of things that have happened, and I just would like to just sit with myself and have my memory back."

Kelsey doesn't seem to know what has caused her memory loss. We wonder if she may be struggling with a mental health issue or some kind of trauma – an accident or an injury, perhaps substance abuse, or some other cause. We don't know, and she does not say.

What we do know is that Kelsey is a kind, gentle, fragile, and beautiful soul who also stands alone on our busy main street medians begging for money. Like a flower sprouting from the concrete, Kelsey waits hopefully for a bit of commuter compassion at a bustling intersection. Bright and delicate, she humbly makes her claim to be noticed.

Reflecting on our time with Kelsey, the following words came to mind:

A beautiful flower sprouts from a cleft of urban concrete.

Isolated, alone without anyone to nurture or cherish this scenic rarity.

No former glory, no mind for tomorrow, just the grand radiance of today.

Briefly here for us to enjoy its lovely floral fragrance and subtle shimmer…

I pray we don't thoughtlessly trample her under our collective feet.

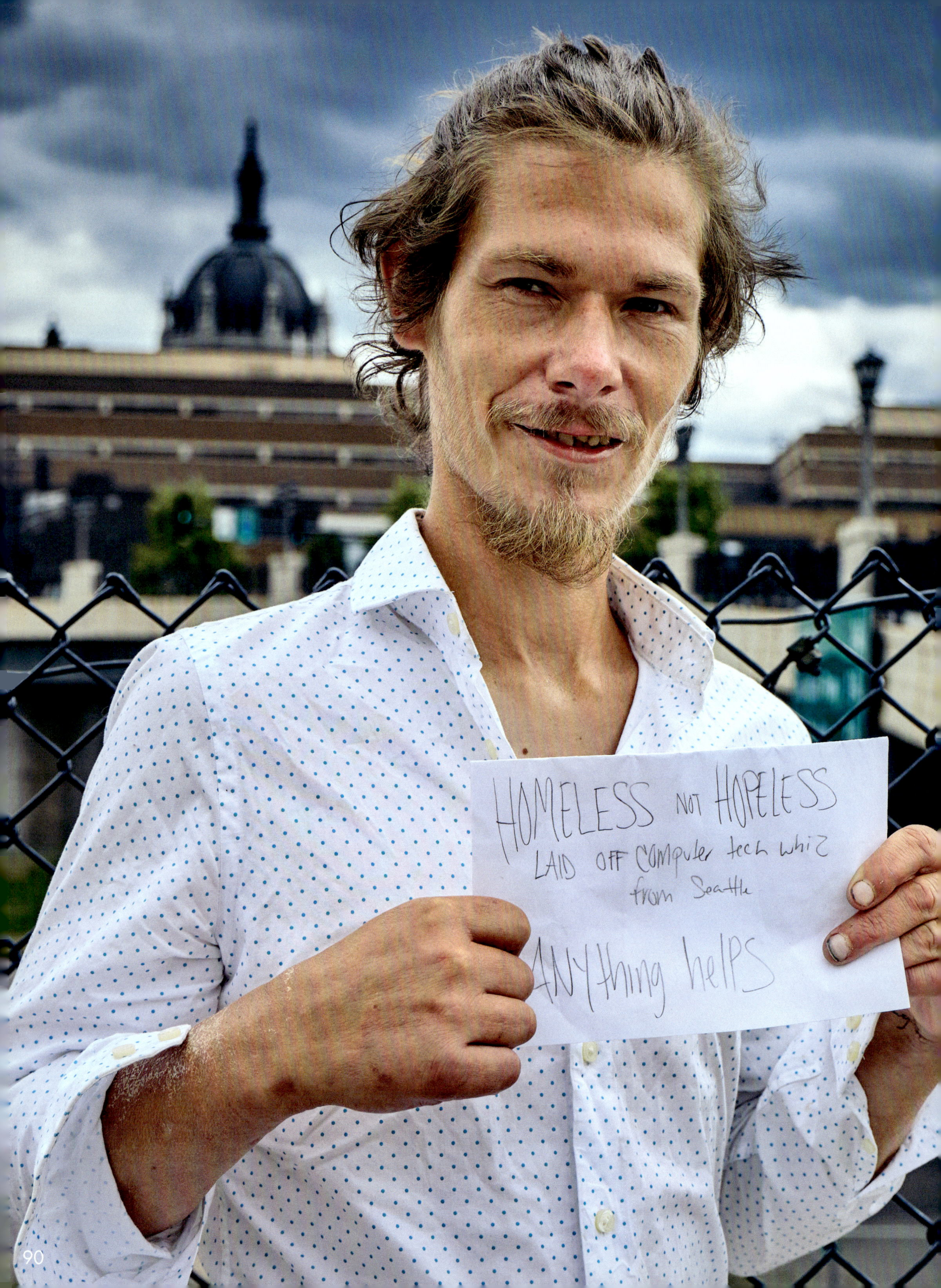
HOMELESS NOT HOPELESS
LAID OFF Computer tech whiz
from Seattle
ANYthing helPS

Kevin K.

Kevin stands on the corner of a busy Saint Paul boulevard. At first glance, he looks distinguished, wearing a long-sleeve button-up white dress shirt with an open collar and rolled-up sleeves. He seems a little out of place, perhaps a corporate executive out for a walk. However, this similarity is quickly lost as he holds a white paper sign. It's barely visible, with text much too small, nearly lost against the background of his shirt. We wonder if Kevin, like his paper sign, will go unnoticed against the background of the busy city as the Saint Paul Cathedral looms over nondescript brick buildings not too far away.

"We try to share food and cigarettes. If someone doesn't have something, usually someone would chip in and try to get it for them."

Kevin's family moved to Seattle from Saint Paul shortly after he was born. His dad struggled with alcoholism and was terribly abusive towards Kevin, his mother, and his brother. At one point, some concerned friends intervened. "When I was, like, in 7th grade, I think, some people from our church came and, like, rushed us to the airport, and we waited in security, because my dad always said he'd come find us, you know?" Feeling unsafe and hunted by one's own father is not a great way to grow up. His dad eventually caught up with them and threw his mom out of a moving truck. She required 72 stitches in the back of her head. Kevin's mother survived and remarried. She now lives with his siblings and Kevin's 16-year-old son, Landon.

As a youngster, Kevin had dreams like every child deserves to have. "I always watched X-Files, and I wanted to be an FBI agent, you know? So, even until the time I was 18, I still wanted to be an FBI agent. But then I got into computers and everything. So, I went to school for computer networking."

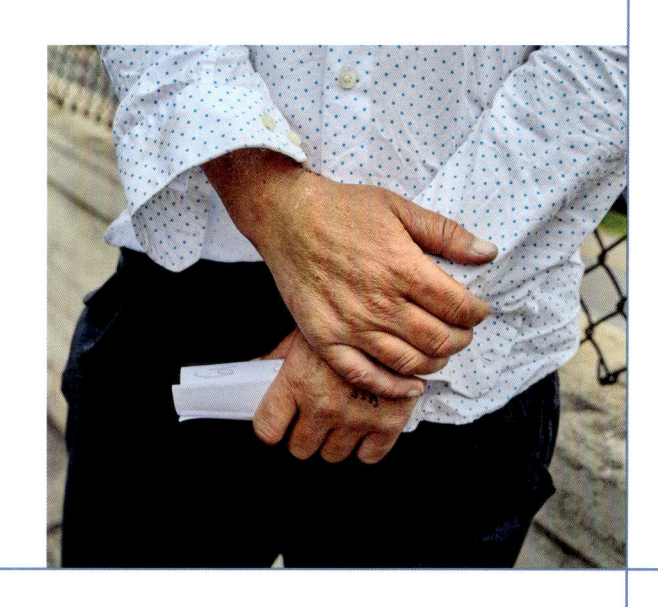

Strangely, while attempting to get his bachelor's degree from Rasmussen College, Kevin was told that the high school diploma he received was from a fraudulent company. It was an unexpected twist that threw Kevin completely for a loop. "Yeah, it was weird because my high school was the one that sent me to this place." He's still trying to figure out what happened, but he doesn't have the means to do anything about it. So, despite claiming to have a degree from Renton Technical College in Seattle, Kevin says he still needs to get a GED before furthering his education. Having experienced some very significant physical traumas now causes Kevin to feel more vulnerable than most.

The initial incident happened during Kevin's time in Seattle. A group of four people attacked him in a grocery store after accosting him for kissing his ex-fiancée on the cheek. Initially, he was grateful, thinking he was not injured. However, he quickly realized he was experiencing severe foot pain and was unable to put weight on his foot. "I broke the bone on the very side of my foot." The injury involved severe tendon damage, causing Kevin to suffer chronic pain and to have difficulty walking.

Contracting spinal meningitis was another pivotal physical challenge for Kevin. "I woke up one day; I had a horrible headache. It was really bad. At the time, it was really hard because they said to make preparations, say goodbye to people, and stuff like that." For perhaps the first time, Kevin had to deal with his own mortality. Facing the real possibility of death had a significant impact on Kevin, as he feared leaving his young son without a father.

Later, a serious car accident and the resulting difficult recovery led to a struggle with substance abuse. While stopped at a red light, Kevin was rear-ended by a U-Haul truck going 40 or 50 miles per hour. He spent nine months in the hospital recovering. "So, I don't know if you guys remember the whole OxyContin thing, where they were just giving it out to people? I was one of those people. So, they put me on OxyContin, and I ended up getting addicted to it, and I went to treatment."

Kevin was sober for almost 10 years when one of his best friends died. "I kind of slid back into it a little bit, but pulled myself back out." Currently, he's not struggling with any substance issues. "Not right now, but just homeless, and trying to get back from there."

We asked Kevin how people treat him. He said, "It's kind of a mixed bag. Like, most people are fairly nice, and then you've got some people that aren't very nice." Kevin has had folks roll down the window and yell at him to 'get a job!' But some people, he said, "just come by and ask if you're alright. Some say, 'Can I pray for you,' things like that."

HOMELESS NOT HOPELESS
LAID OFF Computer tech whiz from Seattle
ANYthing helps

Kevin shared a time when he felt decidedly unwelcome in a local establishment. "I actually went into a restaurant on 7th Street just to ask them if I could borrow a pen to write down some directions. And the lady just looked at me like I was trash or something. And was like, 'get out,' you know?"

When we asked what kind of help would be the most useful for him, he quickly replied, "Food. Clothes. Anything."

It's not only on the street that things are difficult. Finding a place to shelter is always problematic. Kevin and a friend, Chris, hang out together to stay safe and to share resources. Occasionally, they will stay with some friends in a tent community over by the Union Gospel Mission in Saint Paul. They don't have a tent, but hope to get one. They've stayed at the nearby Dorothy Day Center. They also have been to the Safe Space Shelter, where they can stay the night and receive breakfast in the morning. At times, they have slept outside near the banks of the Mississippi River.

Even at a shelter where they seek refuge, Kevin and Chris must be constantly vigilant. "A lot of people like to steal your things. Even in the shelter, you can't leave nothing out, or someone will take it. I think me and Chris have gone through, like, ten phones in just a few months."

Having allies who will have your back – what is called social capital – is important to survival on the streets. Building relationships is essential not only for emotional companionship, but for personal safety as well. Basic community generosity is often necessary for survival among those living on the streets. "We try to share food, cigarettes. If someone doesn't have something, usually someone would chip in and try to get it for them."

Kevin's vision for his future involves starting a small business with his friend, Chris. "We're looking to start a company. It's a print shop, making t-shirts and other designs. Doing graphic design and computer repair and stuff like that."

Kevin's dream of entrepreneurial self-determination hinges on one critical factor – first, finding success in his quest for a stable home. Once he has a regular place to live, Kevin believes everything else will start falling into place.

Laurie M.

All around us, people are walking with purposeful bounce in their step. Enthusiastic throngs collectively moving together, seemingly without a care in the world. It's as if the Pied Piper is mysteriously playing his flute, hypnotically drawing the populace into his unknown lair. Why all the buzz and commotion? We're only a block away from CHS Stadium, home of the Saint Paul Saints, Class A minor league baseball team. The Saints are playing on this bright, sunny afternoon. It's a perfect day for baseball!

"I don't worry about myself as much as I do everybody else. There's a lot of younger girls out here that need some guidance."

In direct contrast to all this hustle and bustle, stationed at a nearby curb, we find a middle-aged woman propped in her wheelchair, holding a white paper signboard.

The woman goes unnoticed by the swarm of baseball enthusiasts as they quickly scuttle past her, intent on cheering for their beloved Saints, unaware they may have just passed by an unsung "saint." In this life, Laurie may never receive the kind of fanfare the Saint Paul Saints receive from their adoring fans. However, Laurie is neither irrelevant nor is she insignificant, particularly to her fellow tent-dwelling companions.

On this bright day, Laurie does what she has become accustomed to doing in life: she blends in. Like a baseball fan, with her sunglasses casually propped on her grayish-golden hair, Laurie fits in and goes mostly unnoticed. Her carefree, engaging smile radiates a certain beauty and grace that goes well with her neon pink tank top. Fair-skinned and bare-armed, this lady is turning lobster red from the sun. Yet resolute in her mission, she's willing to endure the heat and the scorching sun in the hope of capitalizing on the potentially charitable mood of the crowd.

Homeless-Hungry
Please Help
Anything Helps
Thank You &
God Bless
you!
EMBASSY

As we get to know Laurie, we soon discover that people sometimes step over her and frequently step on her, even though she is a gem of a person. She is one of the sweetest souls one might ever have the privilege to meet.

Laurie is a kind person. She is generous and cares for the people around her. She says, "I give my last of everything, sometimes. I've lost 60 to 80 pounds in the last year. And that's because I would rather see everybody else eat."

Laurie serves as a mother figure, more like a guardian angel, for those new to the streets and naïve. "I don't worry about myself as much as I do everybody else. There's a lot of younger girls out here that need some guidance. And I try to talk to them. I try to be their friend before they get too crazy. They're single, and they're younger, so they're kind of, I don't know, they think it's a party time, but they're learning. They've been beat up. They've been robbed. One girl was raped twice… you can't be alone out here."

"I've been through too much out here, and I don't want to see somebody else, especially somebody younger than me that has so much potential, end up out here like this. I'm right down in the trenches with them right now. I see these guys scooping them up. Sending them out for prostitution and beating them up. I have to help to pick them girls up. Because there's nobody out here that will."

We offer Laurie words of encouragement for being there for these girls by sharing Jesus' words: "Whoever gives a cup of cold water to one of these little ones… will certainly not lose their reward." With tears flowing down her cheeks, she whispers, "I needed to hear that."

For Laurie, life on the streets is a daily struggle for survival. She describes a very disturbing and somewhat common incident.

"Blankets are really important because it's really cold out. Even in the summertime, it's really cold at night. And if you don't have shelter and you're out here, and it's raining, you want something over your head. It's a lot about protection. Somebody stole them. They just blatantly stole them while I was sleeping."

We ask where she goes to sleep at night. "Wherever I can," she says.

"Why not shelters?," we wonder. From Laurie's perspective, it's safer outside. "I don't like the shelters because it's worse than being out here. I feel safer out here because in the shelter, you're enclosed, and I was attacked at least three times in the bathroom at the shelter in the middle of the night. It's not safe. They don't have anybody there to protect you. I feel safer outside."

"Last night, I had three dollars. That's all I had from signing yesterday, and a man came and punched me in my face and took it. Living on the street is like the cowboy days. I compare it to the Wild West."

"In the last year, I had three different encounters. Occasions where I was assaulted badly enough that I should not be here right now. And God intervened, and just at the point where it probably would have been too late, somebody would show up."

Laurie has experienced a few tragic turns during her life's journey, and her story is complex. Growing up, she had aspirations to work professionally in the music industry. "I was a semi-professional singer in Nashville for a few years. I used to sing at church a lot. I used to be a leader of a praise team down South."

Music took a backseat when she married at age twenty-one. She has four children, and "I have five grandchildren," she proudly announces. "My biggest concern is I'm going to die out here on the street. I don't want to die on the street. I don't want my grandkids to know me like this. They don't need to even know I'm out here."

Laurie's life hasn't always been this way. She recounts a series of destabilizing, life-jeopardizing events as we discussed what brought her to this street corner. "My ex-husband broke my back 20 years ago. I'm in need of a sixth surgery right now. I also have Multiple Sclerosis and Lupus. Sometimes I'm in remission."

As Laurie continued her tale, the number of tragic turns mounted, one after another. "I rented a room from a man who tried to murder me. My daughter called the police, and they took him to jail. I thought my daughter was taking me to her house, but she dropped me off in Minneapolis and cleaned out my bank account. She was on drugs really bad then. I don't judge her, because I was a drug addict for a lot of years. I've been off drugs, heroin, and crack cocaine for 15 years now. My daughter is off the drugs now, and she's trying to make amends, but she can't change what's already been done. And I've been out here on the streets ever since. It's been three years and I'm not getting back on my feet."

"My biggest concern is I'm going to die out here on the street. I don't want to die on the street."

"I wish everybody could understand that I'm not out here because I'm lazy. I don't want to be here."

As our time together comes to a close, we observe a more vulnerable side to Laurie.

While she finds purpose in helping others, Laurie confided that she sometimes feels overwhelmed and experiences a deep sense of hopelessness. Health concerns and her unstable living circumstances are like a never-ending emotional roller coaster.

The negative public attitudes Laurie sometimes experiences while panhandling have bruised her inner soul. She longs for kindness, yet goes mostly unnoticed. "I wish everybody could understand that I'm not out here because I'm lazy. I don't want to be here. But what I could use is your help, people."

In the distance, fans are gleefully cheering their team and singing, "Take Me Out To The Ball Game," while Laurie sits in solitude, hoping some kind soul will notice her.

"Smile. Just a smile. That would mean the world to me."

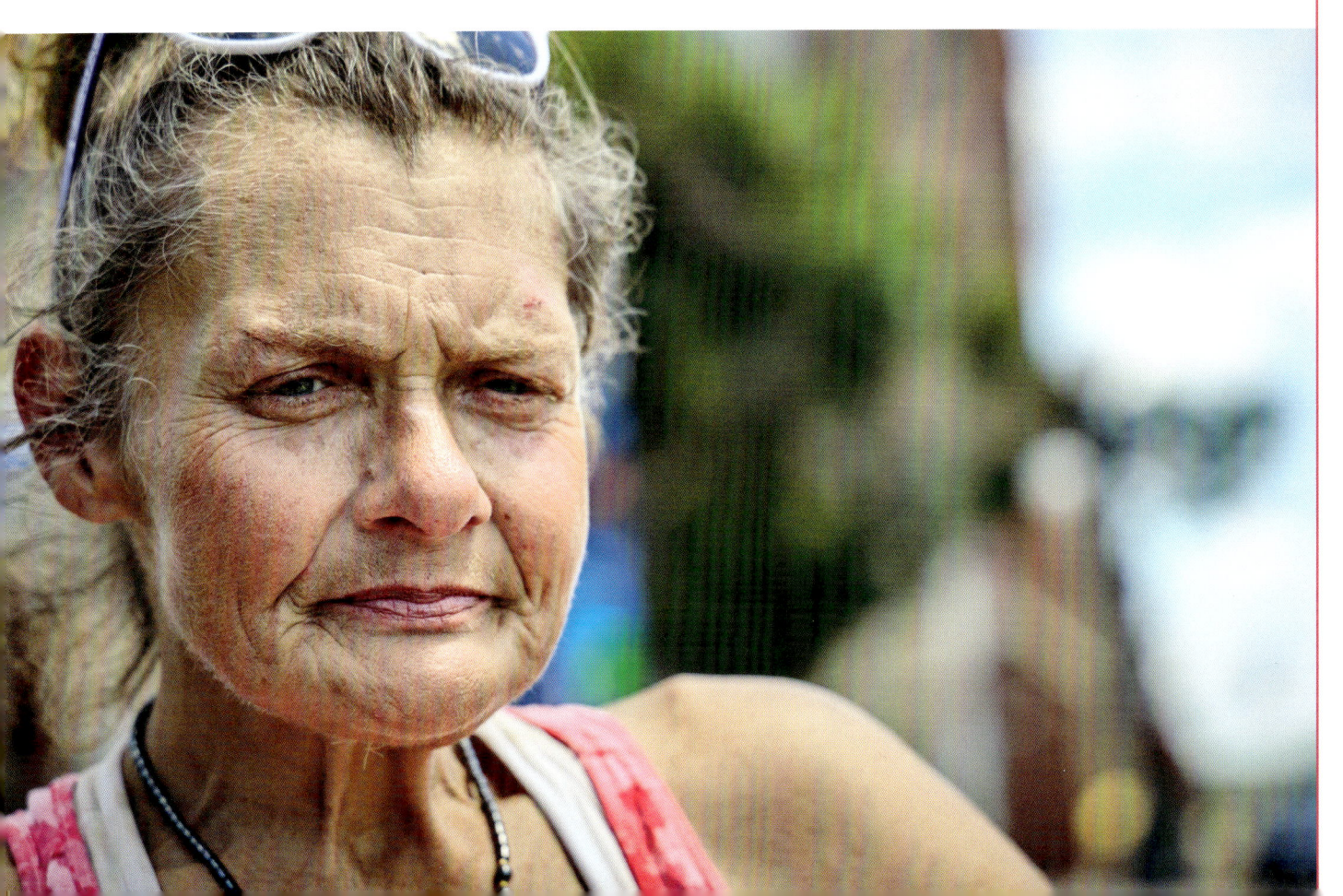

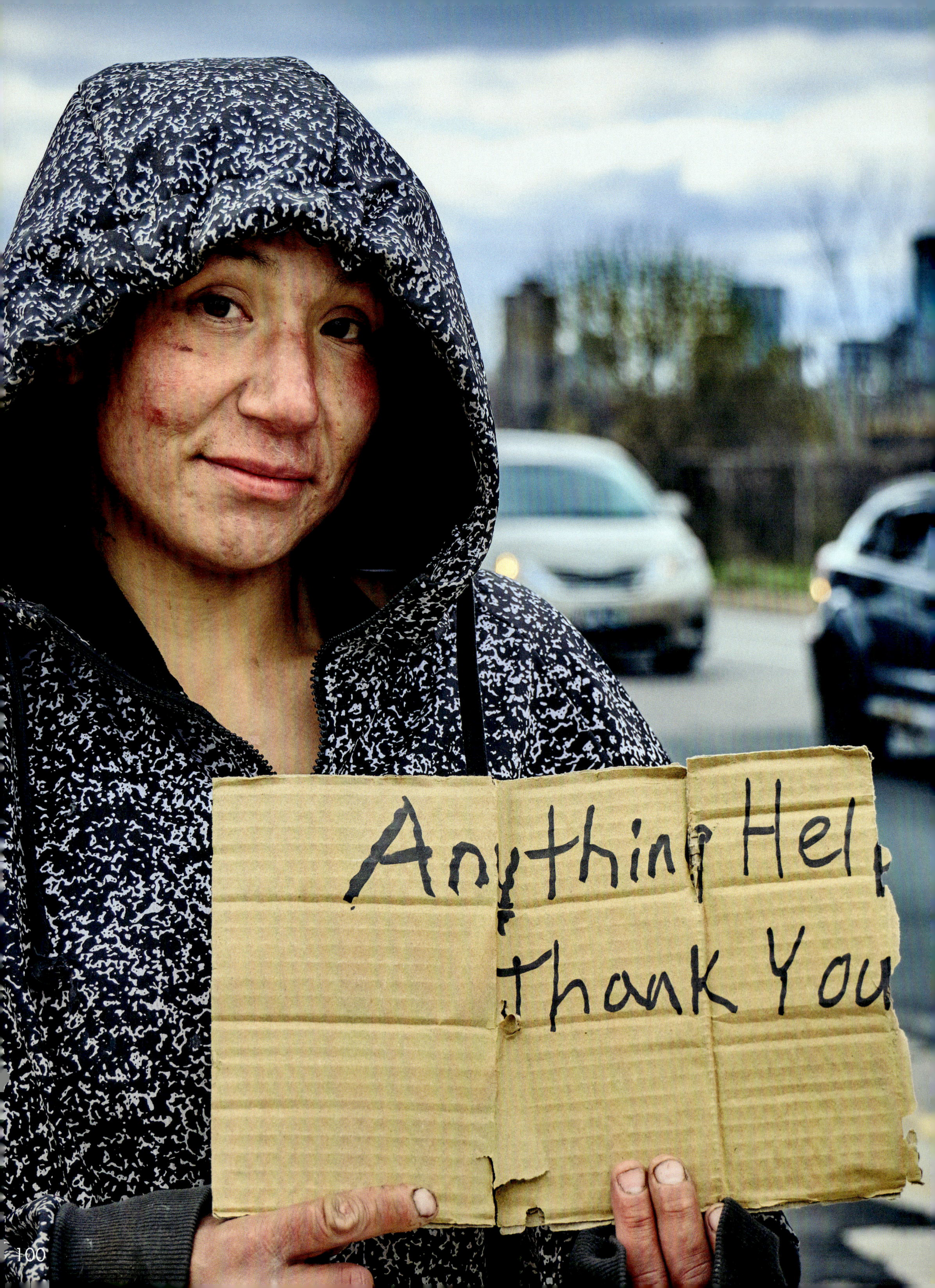
Anything Help
Thank You

Melissa C.

Hidden in plain sight, her slight wispy form and colorless gray outerwear perfectly blend in with the surrounding urban concrete. If we had not been attentive, she might have glided by with hardly a notice, perfectly cocooned in her zip-up hoodie. Melissa is adept at community camouflage and streetwise stealth.

As Melissa shares her story, she displays this same guardedness. She opens up just enough to imply she is a willing participant, but holds back slightly lest she betray her well-honed cover. A bit anxious, Melissa bites her nails and stands propped with one foot overlapping the other, her nonverbal clues offering nearly as much insight as her words.

Melissa has expressive dark eyes. Despite broken and badly worn teeth, Melissa's bashful, sweet smile projects the gentle warmth of human kindness. Her cheeks are blush red and weather-beaten. Melissa wears oversized clothing with a backpack slung over her shoulder. She has rolled up the cuffs of her sweatpants on each leg. Her hands are pulled into her sleeves. We wonder if she does this for warmth, or if it's a subconscious coping mechanism. Perhaps burrowing inside her heavy overcoat is an attempt to feel more secure.

What is hard to miss is the fact that Melissa is shoeless. She has been walking outside on this windy, biting, cold April afternoon with her feet covered only by plain gray socks. She doesn't complain, and she doesn't bring it up. This is her normal, and she doesn't seem to waste any unnecessary emotional energy concerning herself with things she cannot control.

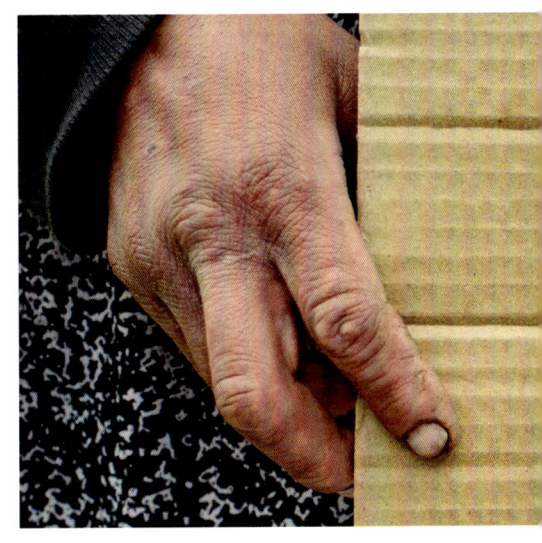

"I wanted to be a boxer. Yeah. Fight."

Melissa has learned to subsist in a space where everyone is typically out for themselves.

A place where the strong survive and the weak die. An unforgiving urban world unwilling to give a break to those not smart enough, tough enough, or resourceful enough. Melissa is tiny, timid, and transient. Being highly mobile is one of her most resourceful methods for surviving on the streets.

Melissa is also a tormented soul, having experienced far more life, death, birth, and living than anyone ought to have known during the brief 35 years she has walked on this earth.

Born in North Minneapolis, Melissa has lived in Minnesota most of her life. Her immediate family is spread out across multiple states. "My dad's still alive. He's in Minnesota. My mom, she stays in South Dakota. I've got siblings that are in different states. Three sisters and three brothers. I just had two that passed away." She is also a mother to four children—two girls and two boys, ranging in age from six months to eight years old. There's so much more we want to know and ask, yet it's clear her family history is a harrowing place for her. Out of respect for Melissa's pain, and to protect her emotional well-being, we hold back from asking more questions about her family that might feel too intrusive.

Instead, we pivot and ask Melisa about her childhood dreams. Surprisingly, she eagerly gushes, "I wanted to be a boxer. Yeah. Fight." One only needs to see her slight frame to know this would not have been a sustainable vocation for Melissa. The irony is striking. Yet, her response offers evidence of the tenacity that exists within her soul. This delicate-looking person radiates a spirit of what the Yiddish-speakers call "chutzpah." It's no wonder she has survived so long with no regular support system.

Melissa conveyed that she has a simple goal. "I just need a job. Something that pays good money. I didn't graduate." Without an educational pedigree, Melissa has a difficult road ahead of her. But if she can harness her fighting spirit, she may find a regular occupation – something that pays enough to provide stability, and at least some semblance of normal.

With her strong spirit and resilience, Melissa has a fighting chance.

Maria T.

An online story recently showed a photo of a tattered handwritten sign that read, "End Homelessness with Mandatory Baths." Thought-provoking? Sure. A bit of a stretch for the imagination? Perhaps. But there may be more to that idea than one might think.

Most of us try to care for our personal space. We clean our home, and we mow our lawns. Hopefully, we make our bed, wash our clothes, shower, brush our teeth, etc. – the regular duties we have come to associate with orderly living. Addressing these basic tasks doesn't cure every ill for those experiencing homelessness, but it does restore dignity and human significance. Basic cleanliness can restore a sense of order in one's life and can be the first building block to regaining the traction necessary to achieve some semblance of "normal."

On a sunny and warm autumn afternoon in downtown South Minneapolis, we meet Maria, a young woman struggling to find her own "normal." She is not the stereotypical image one might have of a person experiencing homelessness, or someone you might see begging on the streets. Maria has a certain light in her eyes, an engaging smile, and clean, carefully styled shoulder-length brown hair. She's sporting a fresh-looking blue top, checkered pajama pants, and black Nike flip-flops. She carries an overstuffed backpack slung over her shoulder. Minding her own business, Maria casually sets up shop at the nearby corner, sliding her backpack off her shoulder and pulling out a small white cardboard sign with multi-colored, tightly spaced lettering.

"Washing clothes helps me to feel good and to be seen."

104

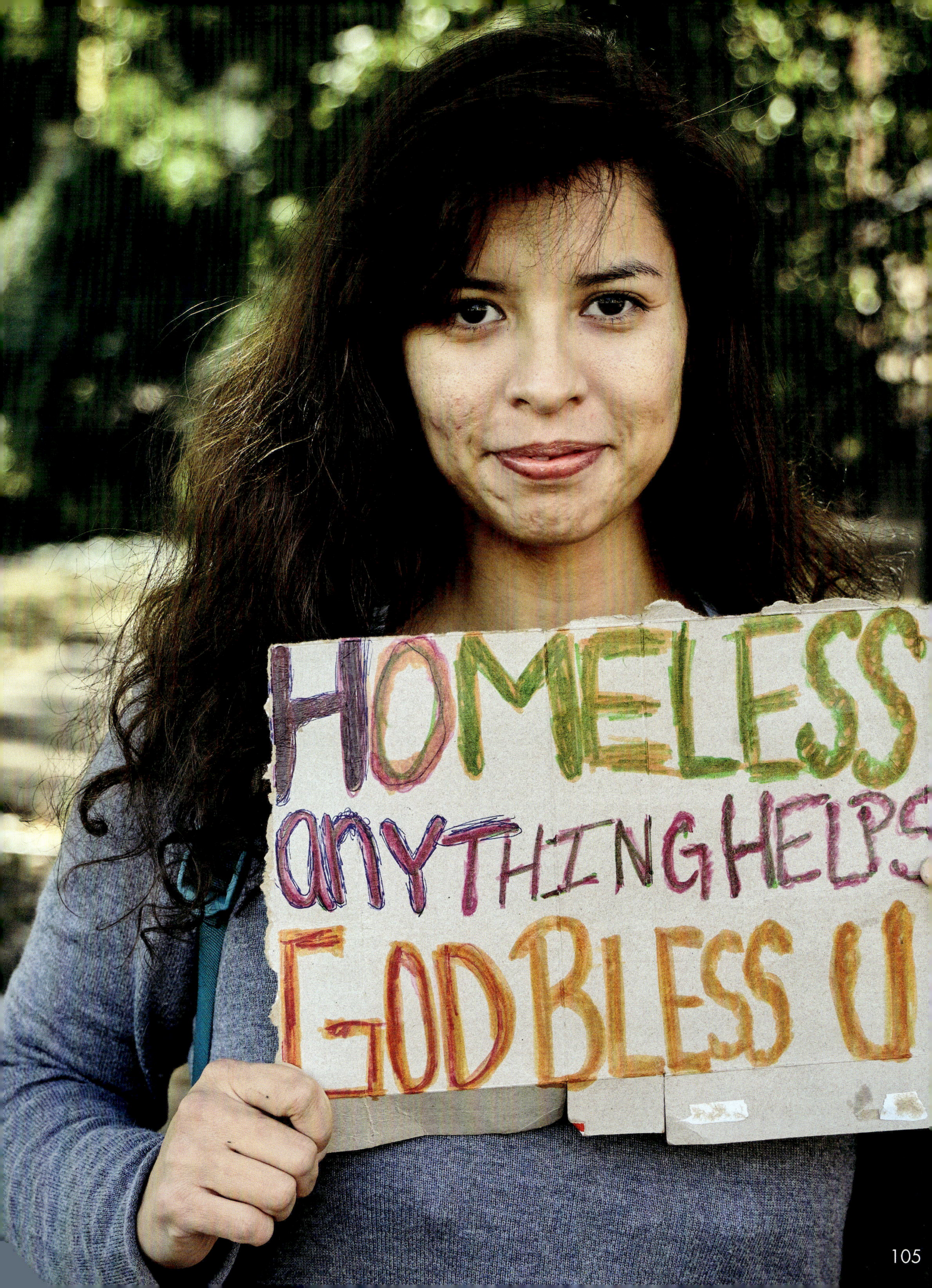
HOMELESS
anyTHING HELPS
GOD BLESS U

As we engage Maria, we soon learn that her life has been filled with a series of intense struggles that have flipped her world upside down. Since she was eighteen years old, the tragic murder of her beloved mother and sister has plagued her with Post-Traumatic Stress Disorder and mental health concerns. Maria is Native American by descent – a mix of Lakota and Ojibway, and claims her uncle was a Medicine Man who used his status to sexually abuse older women residing in nursing homes. All of this trauma and more drove Maria to flee her community and go out on her own, despite the challenges she knew she would face on the streets.

"People pass by me, and they don't want to look at me… it kind of hurts my feelings."

As a young person, Maria dreamed of attending school to become an attorney. "I wanted to be a Lawyer because I like to argue, and I was quite good at it," she shares with a bit of enthusiasm and a glint in her eye. But time and personal troubles have caused her dreams to change. "I got one-third of my business degree with Colorado University online. Little by little, I plan to get my culinary arts and cosmetology degrees done, so I'll be able to have a restaurant with a salon." Maria claims she must first find permanent housing to achieve her dream. "To have my own place to stay because that's my stability. That's how you grow. Stability to build off of, that's all I would need."

For now, Maria's aspirational goals of finishing school and starting a business must be placed on hold, as she attempts to break free of the relentless cycle of living in survival mode. The impending winter and the bitter cold give her significant cause for concern. "It's going to get cold. There's a few shelters that help, like over at the Wakiagun, Avivo, and tiny homes. They have one where you come in at certain times, but you have to leave the next day."

Finding stable housing is undoubtedly a critical need, but it's not Maria's only challenge. "I deal with (substance abuse)… I use, and I also have mental health problems. I can't just quit using. If I were to just quit using it would affect my mental health. I need to get my mental health figured out first before I can sober up. I don't want to keep doing this s**t."

Maria's future is uncertain. She knows it's incredibly dangerous living alone on the streets, and she fears for her safety. She shares, "There's like a new law you can't really sleep outside at night no more, so it's like I'm more or less sleeping during the day than I am at night." Finding a daytime space to catch a precious few winks of uninterrupted sleep is no easy endeavor.

Maria spends most of her time and attention maintaining her basic needs, leaving little capacity to plan beyond her immediate concerns. She regularly frequents a few of the friendlier restaurants to get drinking water and visits the local food shelves for groceries and restroom facilities.

Despite her challenges with time management, Maria has been able to secure employment on occasion, but says, "I end up quitting and sabotaging my future because of my addiction and mental health concerns."

So, for the past three years, Maria has stood at various local intersections with a bright smile and a friendly wave, begging for a living, yearning for some caring soul to take notice and to hand out hope. She is primarily looking for money, but food, water, or even a kind gesture are always welcome ways to fill her emptiness. Some days, she begs for as little as three hours, and on other days, for as long as nine. On Maria's best day, she once made $40 in only three hours. Typically, however, her efforts are not rewarded with such generosity.

Maria says that her circumstances are made more difficult by those who judge her or assume the worst. "People pass by me, and they don't want to look at me... it kind of hurts my feelings," she confides somberly. You know, they give me money but then tell me, 'I know you're going to go use this for the wrong reasons.'" For Maria, the constant barrage of negative comments can be the hardest challenge of all to overcome.

Like all of us, Maria longs for a better life for herself. She understands the value of self care. Maria is grateful for a supportive friend who allows her to regularly wash her clothes. It's Maria's way of maintaining her personal dignity, and removing the stigma of uncleanliness so often associated with those who live on the streets.

"Washing clothes helps me to feel good and to be seen."

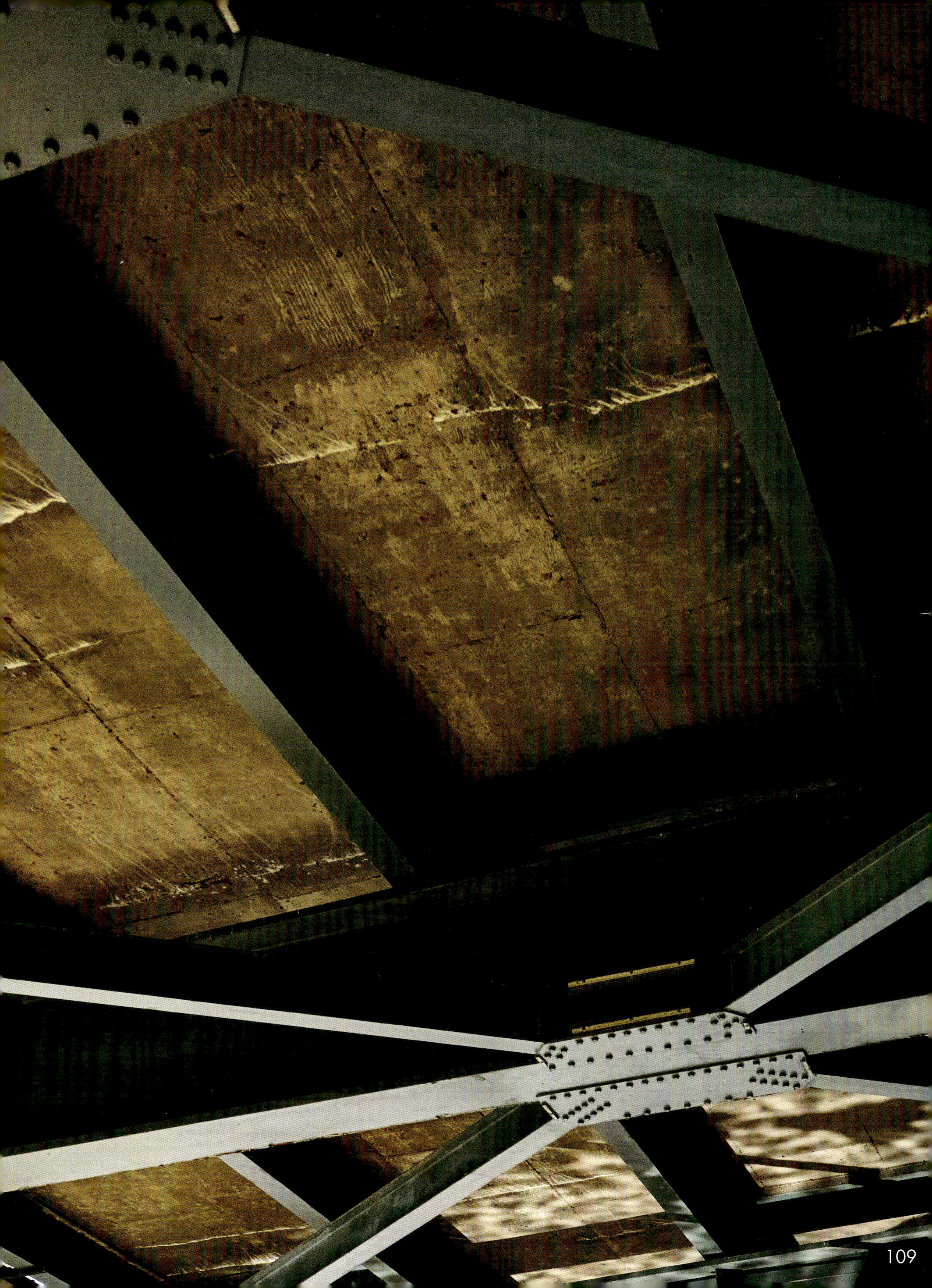

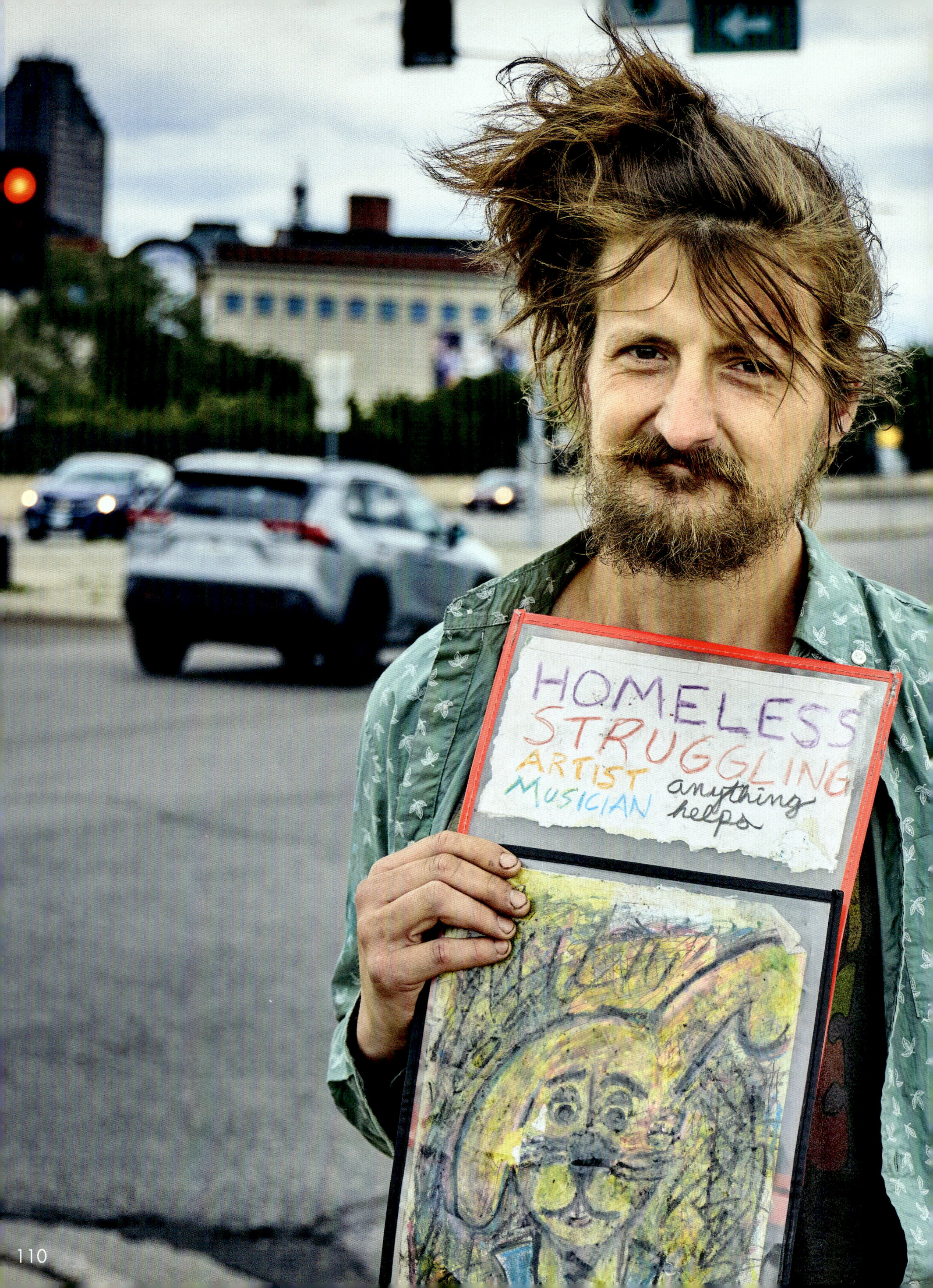
HOMELESS
STRUGGLING
ARTIST
MUSICIAN
anything helps

Paul Christopher D.

Paul Christopher, or Chris as he prefers, is easy to spot on the busy Saint Paul intersection where we met up with him. He sports an ungroomed beard and long dishwater blonde hair slung loosely over his head in a makeshift bun. His eye-catching customized sign includes multicolored lettering and a colorful, almost whimsical, drawing of a rabbit with human features. Even from a distance, Chris's sign stands out against the dull afternoon. Shakespeare once wrote, "To be or not to be." Observing Chris, who clearly has a gift for visibility, we can almost imagine Shakespeare saying, "To be or not to be seen."

Since he was 13, Chris has loved graphic design. When he was younger, he liked to create Anime (Japanese cartoon) websites. Pursuing his artistic passions, he graduated from college in 2020 with a degree in graphic design. His profile on Upwork, where he used to find work on freelance projects, has glowing reviews.

Chris wants to return to making money using his talents, but he says one thing keeps holding him back: "For the hourly jobs, you have an application you must download that takes a screenshot of your computer every 10 minutes to make sure you're staying on track. And I don't have a computer." Once he can get some money together, he hopes to buy a computer from PCs for People.

"Sometimes when I feel like I'm doing well, I'll almost self-destruct because I feel like… I'm not good enough to get where I am now."

Raised in Fargo, Chris attended a private Christian school most of his life. "I definitely believe in God, and I even have a favorite chapter in the Bible, Philippians 4." Most of Chris's family is still in Fargo, but he keeps in touch. His dad has plans to visit him. "I think my dad's actually coming down to see me next week. It'll be the first time I've seen him in four years."

Chris told us his uncle brought him to Minnesota when he was 24. "I wasn't doing too great in 2014 when they dropped me off at the old Dorothy Day with like 20 bucks in my pocket." Despite the rough start, Chris didn't end up on the streets immediately. Chris and his close friend, Kevin, found a place to share in Mankato until they were evicted.

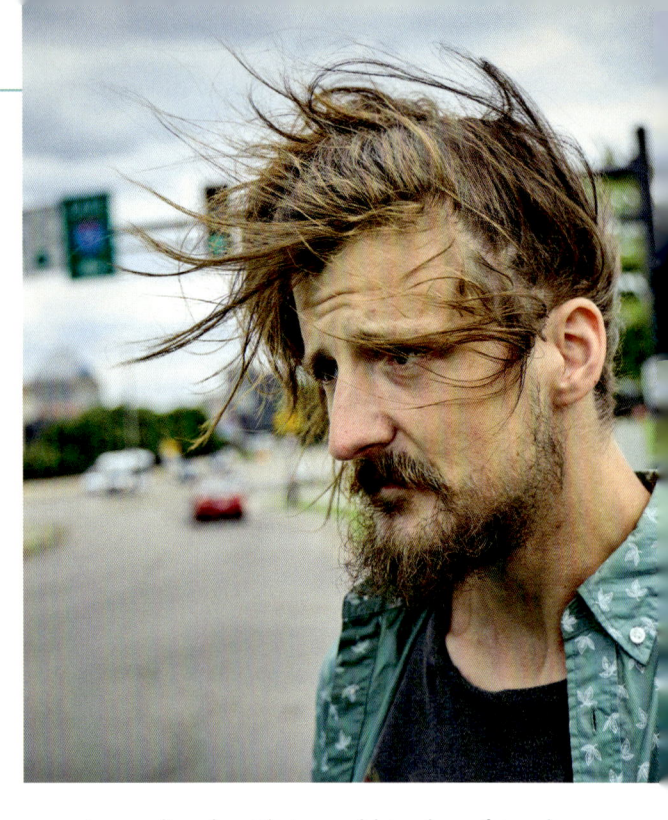

"I was doing great up until about two and a half years ago when I started slipping. I had a good $5,000 in the bank and a car, and then I just started slipping down the wrong path again, and I ended up back where I was 10 years ago. So, I'm just trying to get back on my feet again. My mom died last March, and I kind of spiraled out of control, and so we ended up getting evicted, and then we came back up here in September."

"I like talking to people. I'm not a recluse."

Since then, Chris and Kevin have been bouncing back and forth between the streets and the Higher Ground shelter. "Being on the streets, it can be a lot, and it gets tiring. So, we'll usually be out for three, four, five nights, and then spend a night or two there (at the Higher Ground shelter)."

One of the more difficult parts of living on the streets is all the walking a person must do. "We walk, some days, over 20 miles. I've been walking in these sandals. I got blisters all over my toes and all over my feet right here. So, I put these socks on to kind of help the pain a little bit."

Chris has struggled off and on with substance abuse, using opiates, fentanyl, and heroin. Before the New Year, he started to get back on track. "I'm on methadone. I stopped using, so... It's a little bit easier to get back on your feet when you're not doing that anymore."

For Chris and many of those living on the streets, it's emotionally exhausting to maintain sobriety and find the inner belief necessary to continue trying.

"Sometimes when I feel like I'm doing well, I'll almost self-destruct because I feel like... I'm not good enough to get where I am now."

When it comes to "getting by" on the streets, some days are better than others. Chris' worst day signing, he made three dollars in three hours. His best day was closer to $70 in under two hours. "It's all over the place. There's really no rhyme or reason to it," he says.

Chris appreciates when people stop to talk, even if they can't give money. "I like talking to people. I'm not a recluse." Just having that human connection makes a big difference for Chris. "One time, some lady handed me five dollars and said, 'You know, I see you, right?' I feel like the 'I see you' meant just as much as the five dollars, you know, maybe... probably more."

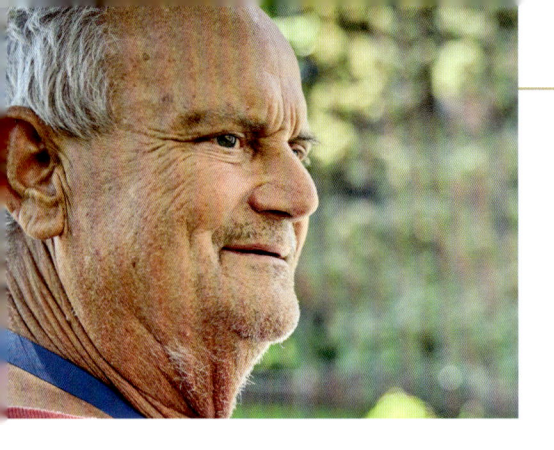

Richard B.

Most of us understand the importance of human connection for our overall well-being. Some experts contend it's a fundamental human need, as essential as food and shelter. These thought leaders suggest that strong social bonds can significantly improve mental and physical health, boost life expectancy, and protect against serious illnesses. For Richard, holding a cardboard sign is more about generating human interaction than monetary transactions.

On this Tuesday afternoon, with the sun shining high overhead, Richard will get noticed whether he wants to or not. He is seated in a wheelchair at a corner near a busy stop sign, wearing a "can't miss me" bright pink t-shirt. He's holding a plain cardboard sign that catches the eye with a simple message: "Thank you." Where one might expect a pity play, Richard projects gratitude instead.

Richard certainly has struggles he could exploit to solicit support. Indeed, it's hard to miss his prosthetic leg. But for Richard, panhandling is not so much about survival as it is about connecting with people.

Richard isn't currently experiencing homelessness. He's just bored. His is one of the most unusual motives for panhandling we have yet to encounter. Richard lives in a nearby assisted living apartment building. He flies a sign, in part, to raise enough money to occasionally go out to eat. "I shouldn't complain, but the food here is terrible," he explains.

For Richard, the pathway to panhandling has taken a unique route, far different than most. As a child, he lived locally with his father, mother, two sisters, and brother. Richard is the baby of the family. He smiles wryly and chuckles a little when he confesses, "Yeah, I was spoiled." His parents have since passed away. His siblings are all alive and doing well, but they don't really keep in touch. "My sisters, they travel a lot. My brother lives in Oregon, and my other sister is in Phoenix. So, we don't talk much. I could probably call them, but I don't know. They don't call me." It seems Richard is simply lonely.

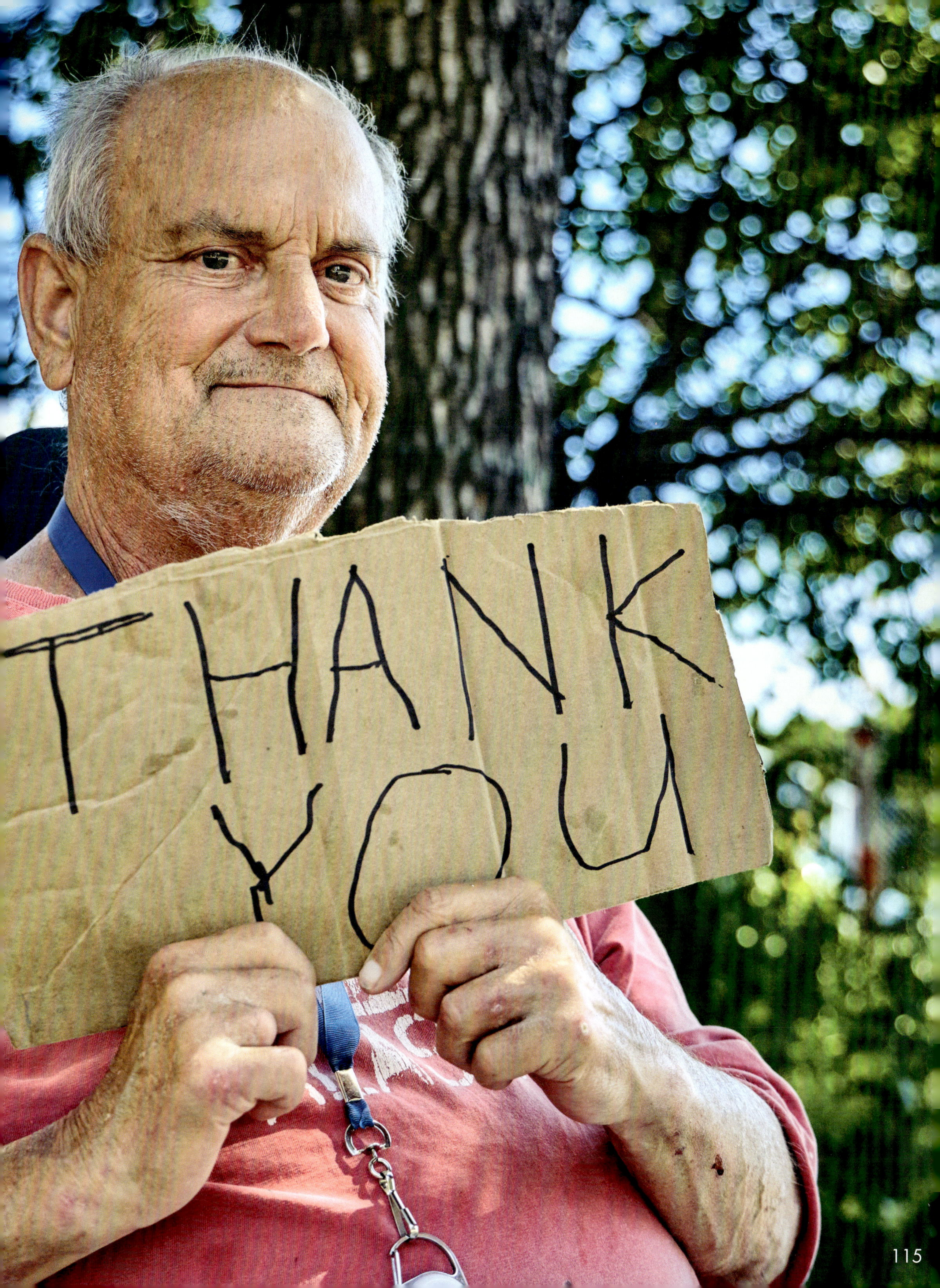
THANK
YOU

"I kind of enjoy it. Some of them just roll their window down and say, 'Hi.' It's kind of nice. Or they say, 'I don't have any money, but have a good day.'"

Richard has held a handful of good jobs over the years. He initially planned to become a lineman at the urging of his father. His dad was a lineman and had arranged for Richard to get a position with Burlington, but he didn't finish the training. "I didn't care for lineman school. I fell off the pole a couple of times. So, I quit. I didn't want any part of that."

For the next 15 years, Richard criss-crossed the country as an over-the-road truck driver. Eventually, tired of the road, he went to vocational school to become a heating, ventilation, and air-conditioning technician and worked several years in the industry. At age 58, Richard became disabled due to complications from diabetes. There's regret in his voice when he admits, "I knew I had it. I didn't manage it very well." He's not legally blind, but sometimes his vision clouds up, making it hard to see. Tragically, Richard lost his leg to diabetes. He summarizes his trauma in a rather matter-of-fact tone, "I got a sore on the foot. Got infected. Went to the bone, and the bone got infected. That happened. Then they cut it off."

So, Richard can no longer work. He lives on a fixed income in a place he does not enjoy. He barely makes enough money to live on, so he sits on the corner of an exit ramp to collect a few extra bucks. On a regular day, Richard will make $50 in three to four hours of panhandling. On a really good day, he can make as much as $150 in the same span of time. While the money is pretty good, for Richard, it's more about social transactions than financial ones. He cherishes his interactions with people he knows, and even some of the new folks he meets. "I kind of enjoy it. Some of them just roll their window down and say, 'Hi.' It's kind of nice. Or they say, 'I don't have any money, but have a good day.'"

Richard is grateful that he doesn't experience a lot of trouble from the other people out here looking for a good place to set up and wave a sign. "If I'm there, they don't bother me, but if somebody's there and you go bother them, they don't like that." So, Richard tries to get out early to secure a spot on his favorite corner. It's close to home and fairly rewarding, both as a side hustle and to fulfill his need for social connection.

Richard's emotional and physical challenges are difficult for him to navigate. When asked about his hopes for the future, Richard slumps a little in his chair and stares off into the distance. He finally mutters, "Not much. Yeah, there ain't much to do here. I go to dialysis three days a week." We ask about the possibility of a kidney transplant, and his eyes glaze as he tears up. Richard replies that he's probably not eligible. His own mortality is a difficult subject.

As we bring our visit with Richard to a close, we offer a simple listening ear and a kind word of encouragement. We ask him if he has anyone to support him. Richard's face immediately brightens as he points towards his friend, Alison, sitting nearby. She offers a warm smile in return. They clearly have a connection and a strong bond of friendship. They may both be struggling, but at least they have one another.

Perhaps it's true, then. Kindness and friendship, vital human connection, can indeed be a powerful medicine.

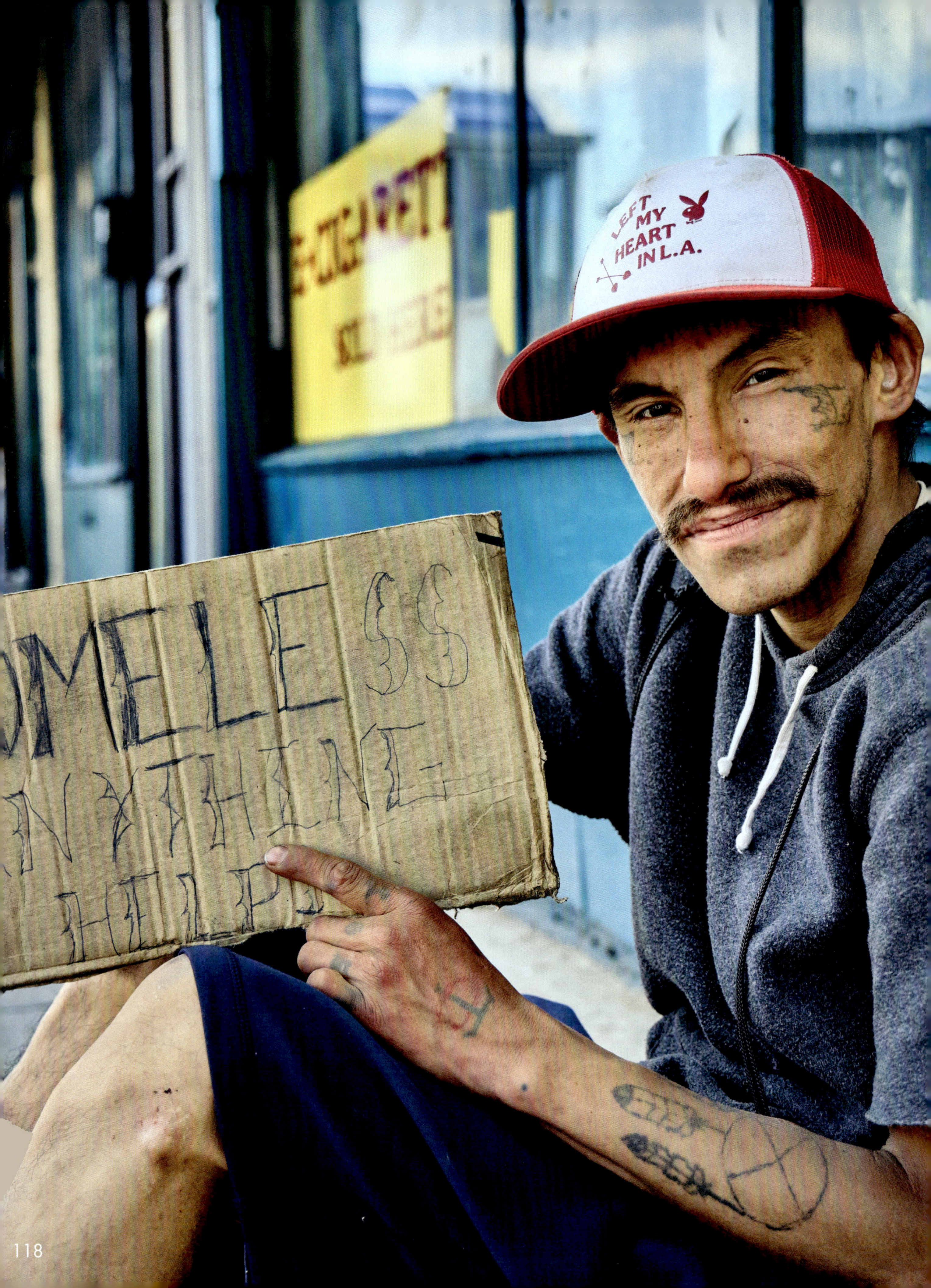
LEFT MY HEART IN L.A.

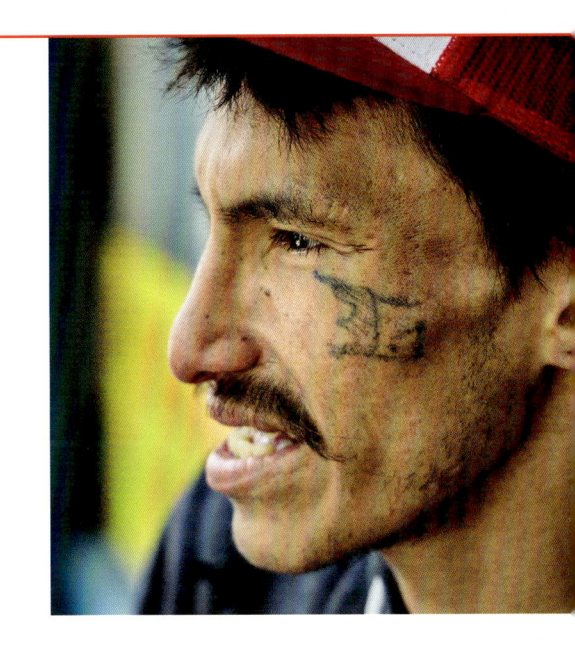

Shane L.

Most of us have experienced disappointment in our lives. Perhaps an expectation left unfulfilled, or a letdown of some kind. Maybe we've fallen short of a long-held goal or aspiration. In some cases, a person can be so close to achieving their dream that they may wrongly assume it will just happen. The disappointment of unfulfilled expectations can be crushing. Without a community support system, such heavy disappointment can completely derail a person's life, leaving them devastated and an emotional trainwreck.

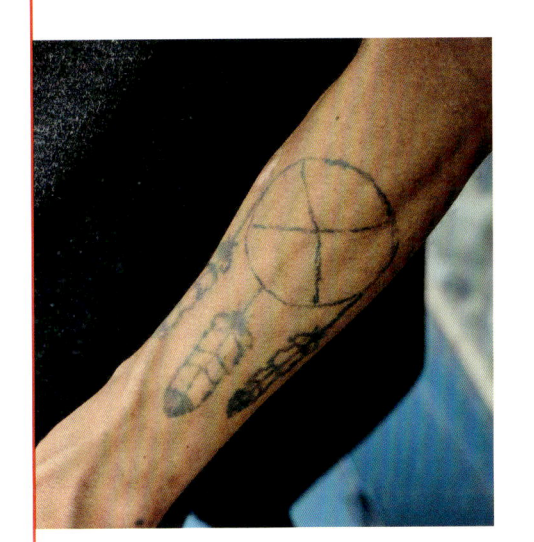

We find Shane in downtown South Minneapolis near East Franklin and Bloomington Avenue. He stands in the median, seemingly unconcerned for his safety, waving his hand-scribed cardboard sign as traffic buzzes by on both sides. No one seems to slow down or take notice.

As the commuters fly past, they have no way of knowing that this sign-holding, gentle soul once had dreams. Nothing too big or exaggerated, really. He didn't want to become the President of the United States or even the President of his local student council. No, his dream was much more modest and realistic: to finish high school in Cass Lake.

"I was only two credits away from graduating. I watched my whole class graduate without me." It was devastating for Shane, watching from the stands as his friends, one after another, paraded across the stage to receive their diplomas. It threw him an unexpected

" I was only two credits away from graduating. I watched my whole class graduate without me."

119

curveball and tragically derailed the plans Shane envisioned for entering adulthood. Shane's humble dream was crushed, and he has been struggling to rebuild it ever since.

"I came down here (to the Twin Cities) to do my GED, and they said I could get my two credits from that school. So, I tried a local virtual high school, and that took me about a year, but it didn't get me nowhere. So, I kind of got discouraged." Disheartened, Shane turned to drugs to numb the pain.

As a kid, Shane once had a dream of becoming a boxer. Regrettably, he couldn't pursue this dream because of a foolish street fight that left him with a broken jaw. Shane had another dream to play basketball. He says he was pretty good at it. But being two credits shy of a high school diploma, playing next-level basketball was not an option. At only 16 years old, Shane became emancipated and had to live on the streets. Lacking adult guidance, he had to figure out too much on his own. So close to his dreams, yet never able to reach the finish line.

These days, Shane usually makes his bed under a bridge somewhere. The cold, hard ground is not a friend to him, but it's what he knows. "I carry around this little blanket just to stay warm because it's cold at night." Day-to-day living is a struggle. His belongings often get stolen.

Shane has not completely given up. He tries to muster the determination to continually put one foot in front of the other with a 'can-do' resilience. To meet his immediate needs, Shane says food is helpful, clothing is necessary, and comfort, even a small pillow, can make his nights better. We all share the same fundamental requirements, but lacking stability and a healthy infrastructure, Shane struggles to fulfill even his most basic needs.

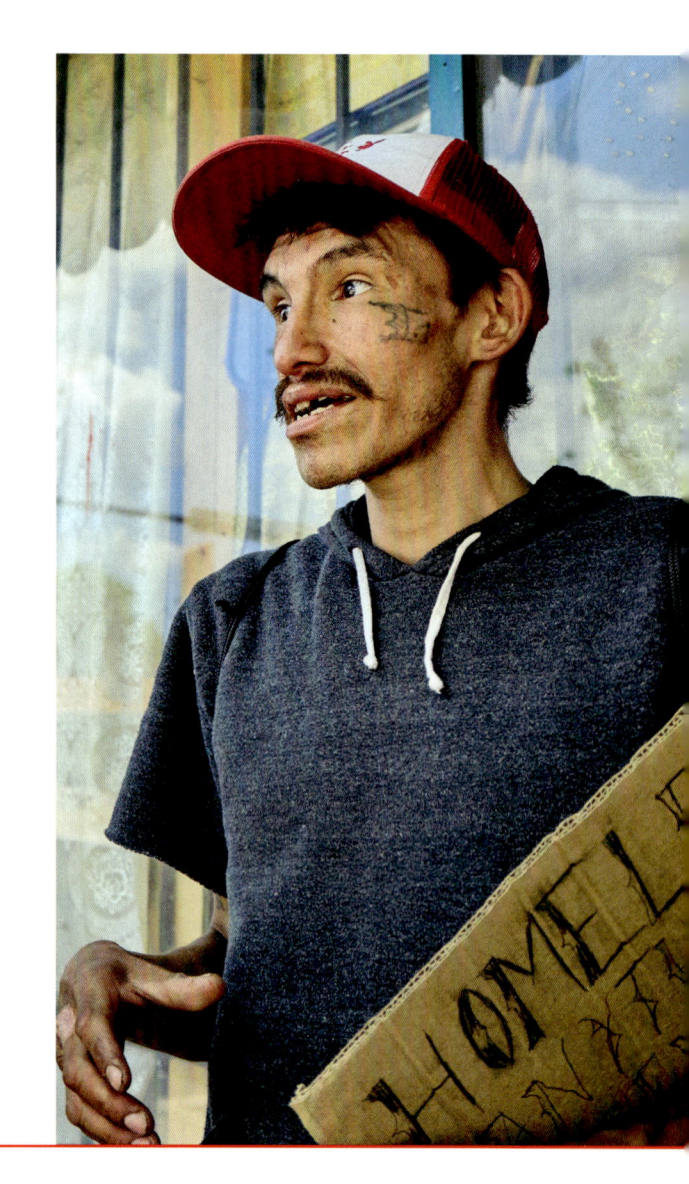

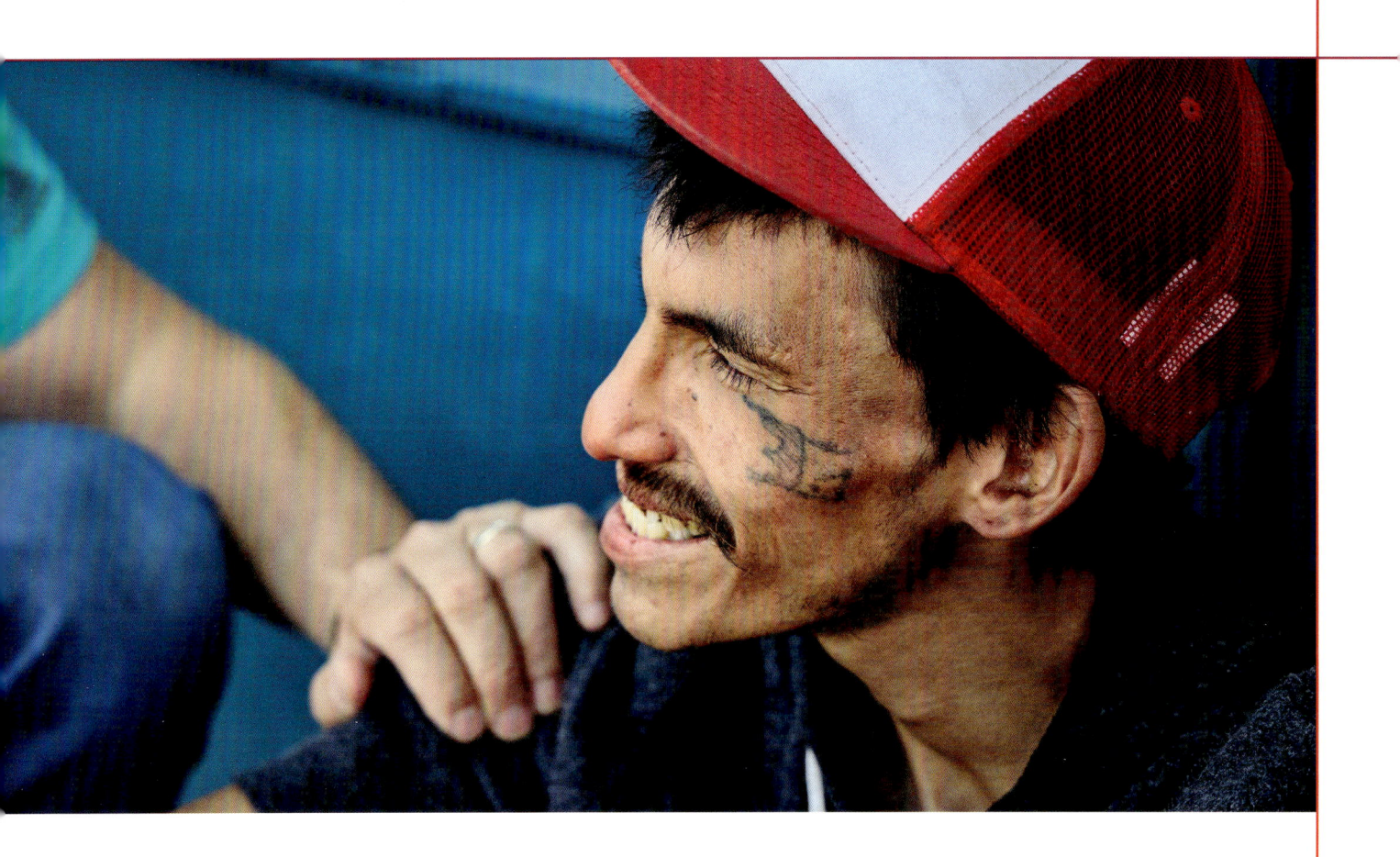

Shane still has dreams, though lingering hopelessness and discouragement are starting to seep into his soul. He thinks one day he would like to get his GED, become a construction worker, and possibly advocate for others. With all Shane has experienced in his life, he still cares deeply for others.

On the day we met Shane, this caring soul was trying to figure out how he could see his 74-year-old mother, who is in the hospital suffering with significant health concerns. Even this basic desire to help his mom presents a near-impossible challenge for Shane. Panhandling is his only practical means of survival, and he has limited money for travel.

The tough streets of South Minneapolis can sometimes feel like a train wreck, but it hasn't completely crushed Shane's heart or derailed his care for others.

He patiently stands on the median, longing to be noticed and hoping a kind soul and a caring heart will offer him a few bucks so he can gather enough for his next meal. Shane's simple sign declares his disheartening reality… "Homeless. Anything Helps."

Thomas I.

Have you seen an angel lately? Would you recognize an angel if you encountered one? It's not a stretch of the imagination to believe that some folks may have seen angels, or in the case of Thomas, someone who may be an angel in disguise. Would it be too much to consider that messengers of light and goodness might be masquerading as sign-holding beggars on our busy boulevards? Spend a few moments with Thomas and you may walk away convinced that you've encountered a modern-day cherub dressed in human skin, though perhaps with a few dents in his halo from life's bumps and scrapes.

Life hasn't been easy for Thomas. Born and raised in Chicago, he lost his mother when he was only two years old. His father remarried, but when we asked how he and his siblings got along with his father's second wife, he uttered, "Oh, my God. Do I have to say it? My stepmother didn't like us. She didn't like me or my brother. I don't know, she just had her issues."

"With God's help, I keep these other guys off the score from robbing these people in this parking lot because they will do it."

Education also proved to be a steep mountain to climb for Thomas. "I have a learning disability: me and my brother. I don't know where it came from. It's just one of those things. I went back to school to try and get my GED. I went there probably a hundred times trying to get my GED, but it's always something different. I ended up doing maintenance work with God's help and blessing. I was good at it. All the jobs that I got were from the temp service."

123

Thomas has no education. No credentials. Just the resourceful skills of a man trying to make a living without the benefits of a regular full-time job. Despite these difficulties, Thomas doesn't display bitterness or resentment. One doesn't hear him crying foul, or "Why me?" He's a person in process who has overcome much, but confesses to having a relentless struggle with crack cocaine. "I was clean for about seven years, and I fell off. So, I got back on. Damn, I got to say this to you. So, I got back on crack. It's hard to get off." His health has become a priority. "I'm going to stop smoking. I've been smoking cigarettes for 53 years. It's hard for me to breathe now that I'm up in age. If I want to live any longer, I better take care of myself."

"I'm a Christian. I have plenty of common sense but no knowledge of books."

We visited with our new friend near the Loring Corners parking lot, clearly a prime spot for panhandling. This lucrative curb is within sight of the Minneapolis Sculpture Garden and its famous Spoonbridge and Cherry sculpture. A medium-sized parking lot separates us from the Basilica of Saint Mary. This busy urban space hosts many unique and diverse citizens representing an intersection of lifestyles. The religious, the poor, the businessperson, the artist, the panhandler, the college student, and people struggling with addictions. It's a hub of activity and a perfect place to capture an audience while the traffic light holds red.

Thomas is an intuitive person who also has a spiritual side. "I'm a Christian. I have plenty of common sense but no knowledge of books." His life has been a journey of survival by simple faith, common sense, and a little bit of help from friends. In 2007, he says, "I was working at One Stop Grocery store, the biggest grocery store in Chicago. And they told me I need to go to Minnesota. I'm being honest…so I came here to get some help because I was on drugs."

Thomas says when he arrived in Minnesota, "It was a snowstorm in the middle of winter. My Greyhound bus was supposed to be here at seven o'clock, but it ended up being here at midnight. I didn't know where to go. But there was some guy at the Salvation Army standing in the doorway. He was waving to me, and he thought I was looking for drugs. He helped me with the right way." Thomas didn't get drugs, but he did receive a warm welcome and some much-needed love and assistance from the local Salvation Army. "They let me in the door to stay there that night, and I got a fresh start in the morning."

Thomas continues to struggle with homelessness and with health concerns, including some severe dental issues and a knee that needs replacement. He has a lifelong learning disability and the constant temptation to use drugs. Yet, Thomas has learned to channel his energy by being positive towards others.

Thomas shared that he's made a connection with some of the commuters he sees regularly. "Some of these people I know now. I enjoy it most of the time. Seventy-five percent, they won't even wave. I don't get mad about it. I make some of them happy by waving. They say, 'Boy, you got the prettiest smile.'"

"Some of these people I know now. I enjoy it most of the time."

Helping others has become somewhat second nature for Thomas. "With God's help, I keep these other guys off the score from robbing these people in this parking lot because they will do it. Like when the parking lot is filled up on Sundays, and they ride through here and they're trying to pull the door or break the windows. I walk back and forth, back and forth, back and forth. Yes, I do that. They know I'm watching." We quickly commented, "You're like an angel of protection for the parking lot." He smiled, and his face warmed with satisfaction. He seemed glad to be validated and recognized for a job well done.

So, what does a modern-day angel look like? Perhaps just like Thomas, a kind man who serves as the self-appointed volunteer parking lot security guard on Sundays. A humble man who brings joy to local commuters with a charming smile and a cheerful wave to brighten their day.

Angels come in many disguises.

Have you seen one lately?

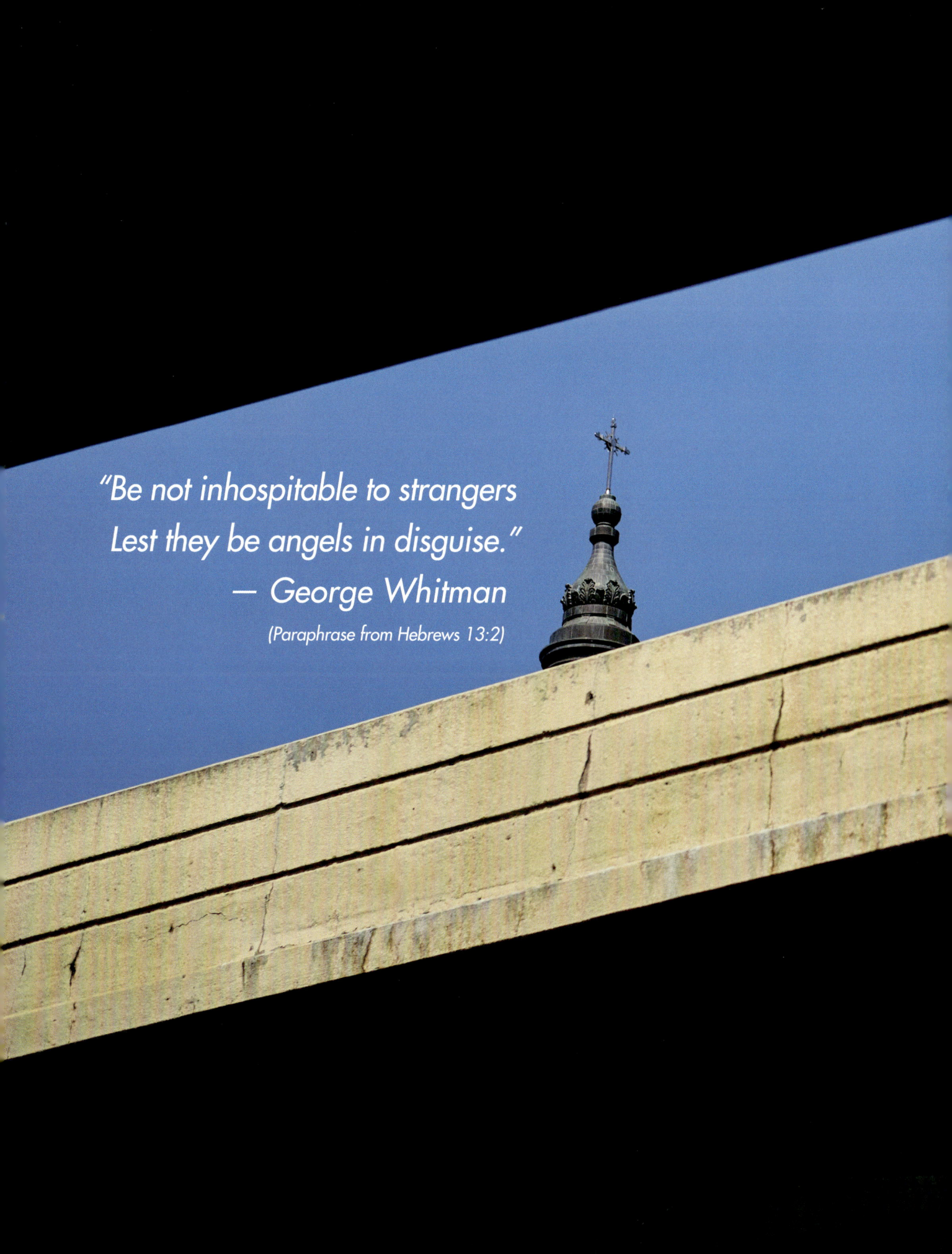

"Be not inhospitable to strangers
Lest they be angels in disguise."
— George Whitman
(Paraphrase from Hebrews 13:2)

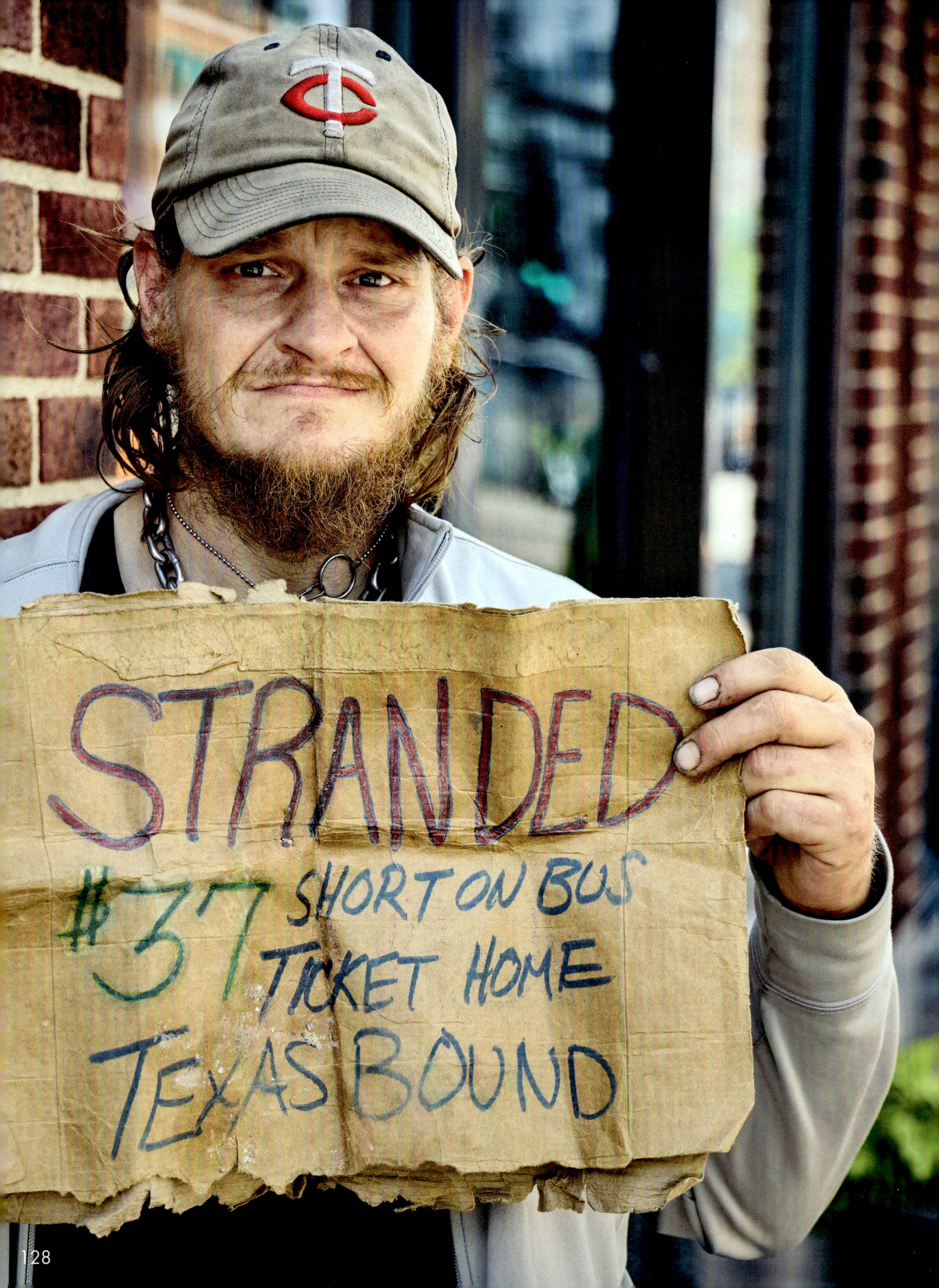
STRANDED
#37 SHORT ON BUS
TICKET HOME
TEXAS BOUND

Tim N.

On a busy city corner just across the street from a major sports arena, we happen upon a dispirited-looking man, Timothy, or Tim, as he prefers. He's holding a tattered-looking brown sign with an oddly specific note scribbled on it: "STRANDED. $37 SHORT ON BUS TICKET HOME. TEXAS BOUND." It's as if he is saying, "Texas or bust." It's most likely going to end in a bust. Why Texas? And why $37? Is Tim a huckster hoping to induce money from those passing by? Is he really going to Texas? Will he revise the amount needed for bus fare after someone extends to him some monetary pity? These are likely only a few of the things one might wonder after encountering this transient sidewalk grifter.

It doesn't require a detective's observational skills to notice that Tim has had a rough life. His grimy baseball cap covers long, unwashed hair matching a straggly reddish beard. He has several tiny circular welts all over the skin of his hands. Are these scars from self-induced cigarette burns, or is he the victim of some form of terrible abuse? We don't know, and he doesn't share. We can only imagine what he has gone through.

"I was sort of raised everywhere. My mom said two kids was too much for her to raise.

So, she got rid of her oldest. I was in 52 different group homes, and 32 different foster homes."

129

With a timid, beaten-down demeanor, it's plain to see that Tim is a deeply wounded person. He seems to be hoping… longing… perhaps even begging for love and acceptance.

Born in Ohio, Tim was rejected by his mom at the tender age of six, and he became lost in the foster care system. "I was sort of raised everywhere. My mom said two kids was too much for her to raise. So, she got rid of her oldest. I was in 52 different group homes, 32 different foster homes." Tim said he remembers the pain of this time in his life, "Every day. It keeps me going." Lacking a normal childhood. No family. No long-term friendships. Like refuse cast adrift in the sea of an overwhelmed system, where child after child is shuttled from one temporary home to another. For Tim, the message that he was unwanted burrowed deep into his soul.

At age 18, Tim became a legal adult and was forced to hit the streets to fend for himself. This has been his way of life ever since. Tim became visibly choked up during our time together, overwhelmed by emotion. He struggled to verbalize his feelings of pain and loneliness, but finally, he said, "I can't find friends out here."

Having goals or imagining a better future means little or nothing to Tim as he wanders daily in constant survival mode. We ask what is most painful for him, and he blurts, "Losing everything and having to start over every day. ID's, electronics… Yeah, my ID is gone." To get into a shelter without an ID requires a community card, "But you better hope you got your community card before they stole your ID."

On the street, danger is all around, even in the shelters, and a person's expected lifespan is somewhat abbreviated. "I've seen so many people get hurt out here. People die out here every day. Sleeping on the sidewalk."

Tim openly shares that he can make nothing, or as much as $150, in six to eight hours standing on the corner. It means he must endure those mean-spirited few who scream, "Get a job!" He says. "They cuss me out all the time. Everything that everybody's used to having, we don't have." Tim says it would be very helpful if those who care and cannot give cash would give items like clothes, sleeping bags, or tents. And food, of course. "Just things to snack on. Food. Definitely water."

The library is one of the few public places where a person can find free access to facilities or a drink of water.

It is always a long walk to get access to the resources one needs most, and Tim's daily steps are many. "The only time I stop is when I go sit down to eat… literally walking from the time I wake up to the time I go to bed." All those miles in worn-out, poorly-fitted shoes and rotten, wet, or worn-out socks have devastated his feet. Tim also suffers from painful back issues and wishes he had a good chiropractor.

For Tim, this is a hard world of unrelenting anxiety, pain, poverty, and rejection. With a pleading voice, he says, "Don't judge us before you hear us." Sadly, he claims, "They don't even acknowledge we're here."

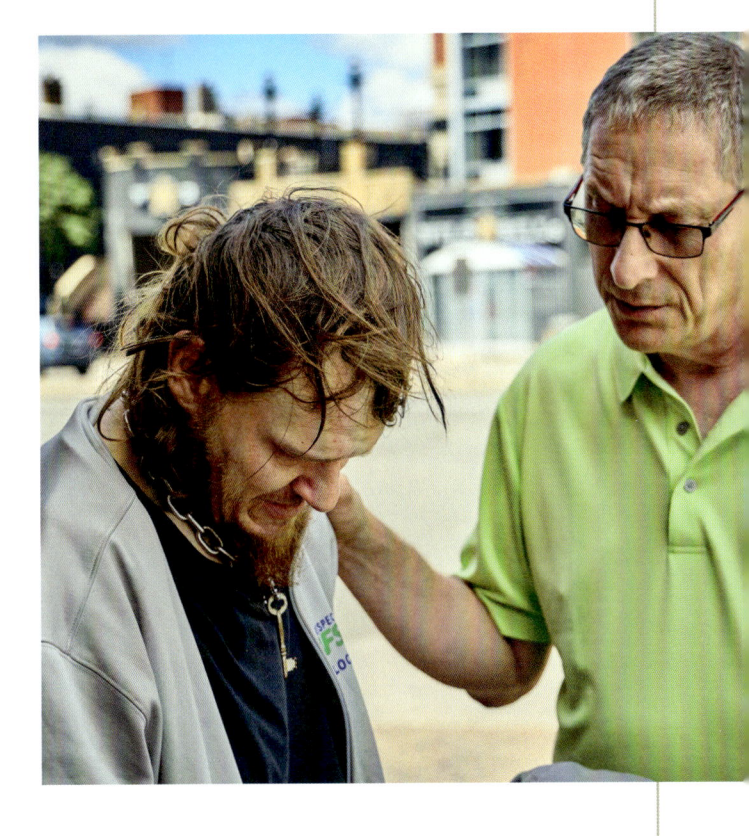

Like so many other transient people, Tim feels insignificant, an unwanted nobody. He is one of the multitude of despairing souls that traverse from place to place on our city streets like modern-day lepers. Rejected, ignored, often slinking in the shadows, just longing to be accepted. Their desperate desire for validation is the fruit of an entire lifetime without healthy attention or affirmation.

One could stand back and judge their indulgent "gimme, gimme" behavior. Or, one could choose to respond with understanding and compassion. How do we do that? By intentionally showing respect and treating others with dignity, regardless of their messiness. Metaphorically speaking, this means setting the relational table with our very best place setting, inviting the unloved and unwanted to sit at the banquet of human belonging. This morsel of love served to a soul starving for acceptance may very well enrich and nourish their lives for years to come.

As we look again at Tim's tattered sign, our questions remain. Will Tim ever get to Texas? Will $37 change his life? It's unlikely. What is real, however, are the tears of a shattered soul and Tim's longing for our society to see him as a person, someone with intrinsic value as a human being. In this instance, Tim's plea may be a clever bit of survival-driven scamming — a stew of mixed motives and doing whatever he can to get cash. Most of us can probably relate to sometimes having mixed motives and occasionally acting with questionable methods. We're human, after all.

"The only time I stop is when I go sit down to eat... literally walking from the time I wake up to the time I go to bed."

As an afterthought, we ask Tim about the chain necklace and skeleton key he wears around his neck. He briefly pauses to gather his thoughts and choke down his tears. It's clear this is a deeply emotional moment for Tim and something of great significance to him. Finally, he whispers a cry of compassion for all children who may be going through the same painful things he's endured, "I've been locked up so long... I just want the kids to be free."

133

Wade S.

As Wade stands at the corner waving his sign with a quiet determination, his gaze follows passersby with a mix of hope and resignation.

Wade's weathered cardboard sign stands as a silent storyteller of his life's journey. Every word, crease, and tear on the sign is a testament to the trials he has endured. It paints a poignant picture of a man who has selflessly served his country, weathered heart-wrenching losses, and now grapples with health challenges. Wade's anguish is deepened by a devastating fire that recently consumed his home and obliterated his beloved toy business.

"I've been blessed. There's still some wonderful people in this world."

The street hasn't always been kind, but Wade doesn't let it get him down. "Some people say 'get a job,' but they don't realize the whole story. You know. 'Get a job, but no thanks for your service.' Not a lot of people even read the sign. Yeah, most people just don't even look at you. They go right by or ignore you purposely. Or they wave. I don't mind that. At least they acknowledge me that way."

The words on Wade's sign tell only part of the story of a man who embodies unwavering faith amidst life's harshest blows.

If one were to pause and truly see Wade's sign, one would notice a single word shining brighter than the others: "Thanks!!" This simple expression speaks volumes about him, revealing not just gratitude, but a spirit of selfless generosity.

Like any of us, Wade is more than his circumstances. Despite facing unimaginable setbacks and personal storms that would break most spirits, Wade remains anchored in thankfulness. He reminds us that gratitude can be found even in the bleakest moments.

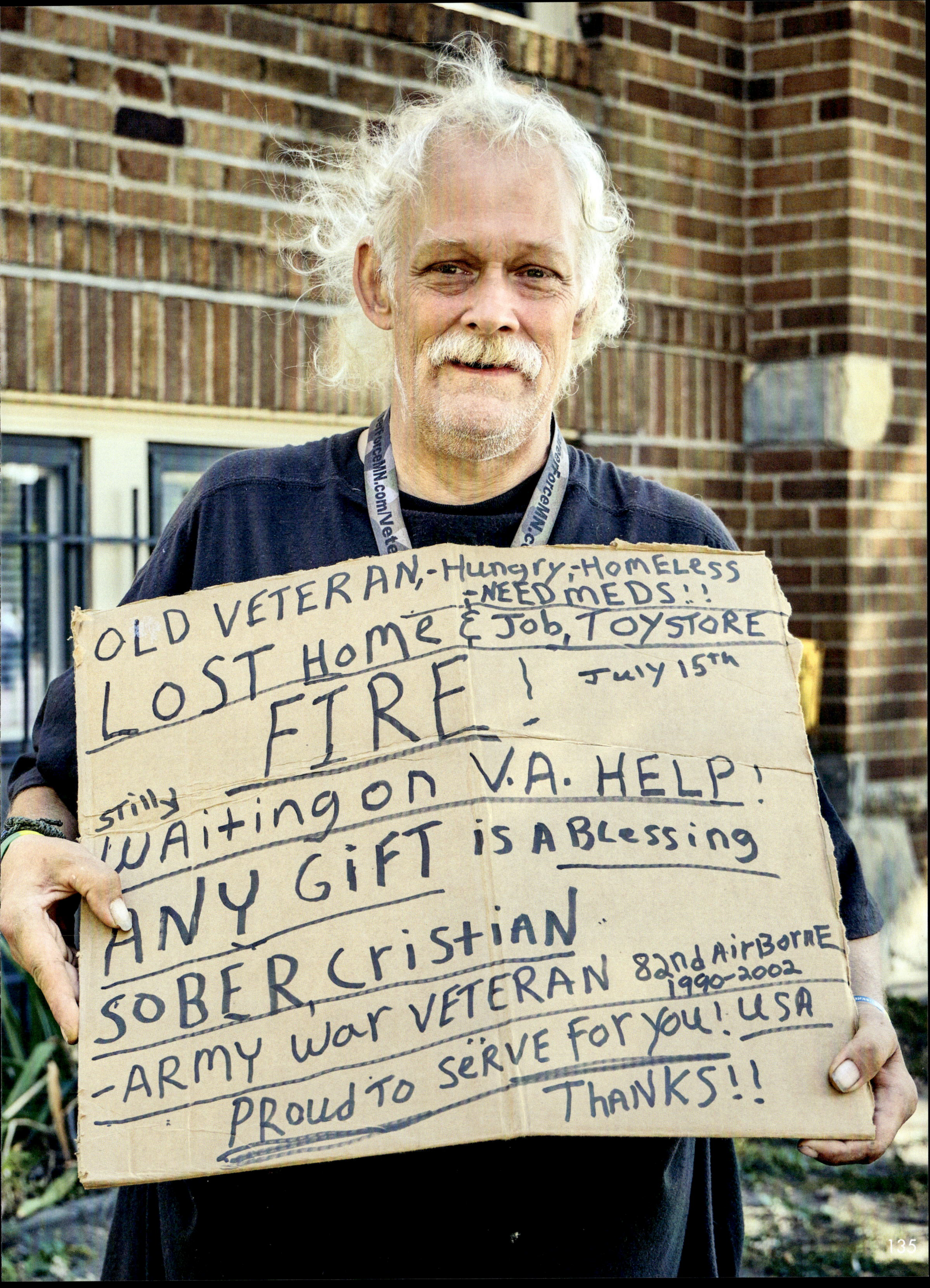
OLD VETERAN, - Hungry, - HomELess
- NEED MEDS!!
LOST Home & Job, TOYSTORE
FIRE! July 15th
still WAiting on V.A. HELP!
ANY GiFT is A BLessing
SOBER Cristian
- ARMY war VETERAN 82nd AirBorne 1990-2002
Proud To serve for you! USA
THANKS!!

A Hero To Remember

Wade's upbringing unfolded against the backdrop of a tranquil resort nestled on the shores of Lake Mille Lacs in central Minnesota, a haven where his mother and grandparents poured their love into shaping him. The legacy of his father, a Vietnam veteran wounded in 1968, loomed large over their family. Despite the life-altering injury that left him with paraplegia, Wade's mother remained faithfully by his side.

The shadow of his father's disabilities did not tarnish Wade's admiration for him; if anything, it fueled his own aspirations to emulate his father's selfless and determined spirit.

As he navigates the complexities of his past, Wade finds solace in the enduring love that shaped him into the person he is today.

"As far as I'm concerned, my dad's the biggest hero in the world. He was a patriot. We didn't have much of a father-son relationship growing up because he couldn't. But we still did things. I still went out with him to the mall for a beer and stuff. But, yeah, my dad, he's my hero."

"I know my blessings are real."

Wade's loyalty and deep-rooted love for his parents is particularly evident in the sadness that flickers in his eyes when reminiscing about the period he took on the role of his mother's primary caregiver.

"I came back home, my mom started getting ill, and I took care of my mom. Basically, I was like a home health aide for my mom. She needed me and stuff like that, and that was that. I came home and took care of her until she passed away. Yeah, well, she took care of me, and I got to take care of her in return. But I don't look at it as a sacrifice. I look at it as an investment."

In Wade's eyes, his caregiving transcends duty; it embodies his parents' legacy of love, an unbreakable bond that continues to shape his perspective on sacrifice and devotion.

"I love making people laugh."

Advancing Amid Adversity

Recently, Wade's life took an unexpected turn when a fire destroyed his business and ravaged his belongings. He lost all of his possessions, and the VA has been slow to provide support. "I pretty much lost everything. And I had my own business. I was doing toys. I sold toys online. I lost everything, yeah. But, you know, a couple of clothes and stuff like that. But I got out with my life. I didn't lose everything. I lost my belongings."

While there have been downs, there have also been some blessings. "Well, my best experience, basically, is when somebody stopped their car. Took me out to eat. Gave me $20 and their phone number. They told me if I ever need a ride to a place or whatever, and stuff like that. So, yeah, I've been blessed. There's still some wonderful people in this world."

Suffering from asthma, allergies, and COPD, Wade is acutely aware of the value of time. "We don't know how much time we have. That's the most valuable thing you got on this earth. You can't get any more."

Wade contemplates the future, and a bittersweet smile plays on his lips. "I know where I'm going," he murmurs, pointing towards the sky. "(Heaven is) Better than here, you know? I get to see my family again." In a moment of shared levity, we playfully caution him not to "take his promotion early." Wade paused and responded solemnly, "I thought about that, but you know what? There's nothing that I can do to kill me. Yeah, I'm looking forward to it (heaven)," he said with a mixture of peace and a longing for what lies beyond. He seems to have made peace with his past and future.

The moment's gravity dissipates swiftly. In response to an inquiry about his support system, Wade beams, "I've got a couple friends, but, you know, higher power. That's where it's at. It took me a while to realize that, but things happen for a reason, and I know my blessings are real." Wade exudes gratitude with every fiber of his being.

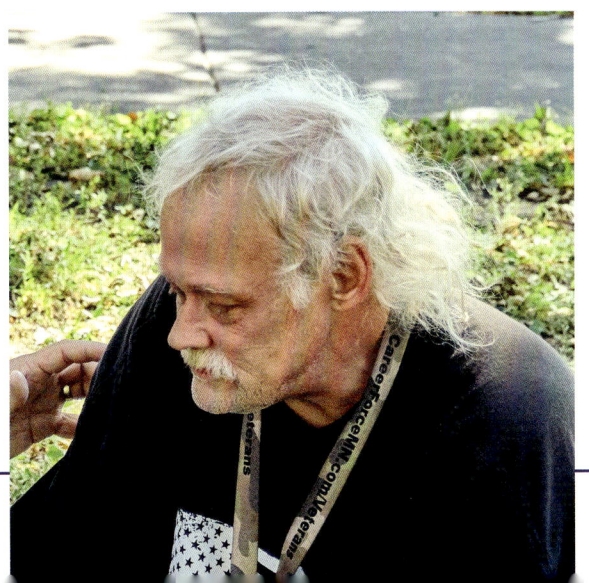

Future Aspirations

As he envisions his future, a radiant enthusiasm colors Wade's expression. Wade's eyes gleam with a flicker of hope and determination, mirroring his patriotic spirit. "Yeah, I think I, you know, I'd like to see things normalized. I'd like to see Americans taken care of first. I'd like the country to be more patriotic. Be the United States rather than divided states." he articulates with conviction.

"My dream is to basically get a grant or a loan to get some property up north. Call it Patriotic Pines and have veterans that come out and get benefits set up for them so they don't go right out on the street," Wade shares earnestly. His dream embodies a personal goal and a mission fueled by empathy and understanding. "That's why we have a lot of problems. That readjustment is really hard. That's really what I want to do, and I think I can do it," he concludes with unwavering resolve, reflecting the weight of his commitment to making a difference in the lives of those who have served their country.

The expectations that Wade holds for folks who pass him by are also very reasonable. "Just be honest if you can't help. At least acknowledgment, you know? 'Thank you for your service. Good luck to you. I'll say a prayer for you.' You know, just acknowledging and realize there's a problem."

Despite health concerns and missing several teeth that make eating solid food a challenge, gratitude infuses Wade's every word, a quality that resonates deeply with anyone fortunate enough to cross his path. In his presence, one can't help but feel the warmth of his spirit and the sincerity of his appreciation. Wade embodies a rare blend of humility and resilience, a testament to the strength found in gratitude.

Wade smiles and laughs frequently. With his jovial nature, it is no surprise that Wade once dreamed of being a comedian. "I love making people laugh. You know, and it's the stupid little things in life that people overlook that are funny. But then we gripe about things, you know? So, it's just a catch-22. Where the humor and the sadness meet, you know? There's nothing better than making somebody laugh. I'd rather kill somebody with kindness and laughter than beat them up."

This dream is a reflection of Wade's heart. Despite all the challenges to his health and stability that he faces daily, his authentic joy comes from giving to others.

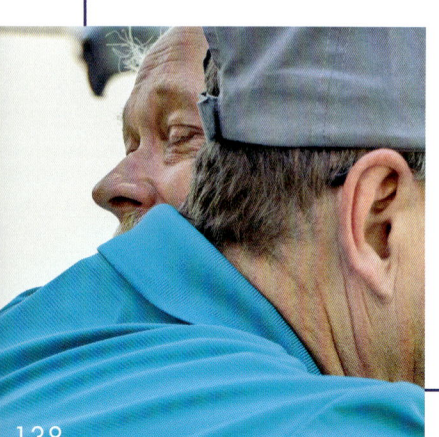

MITÁKUYE
INDINAWE

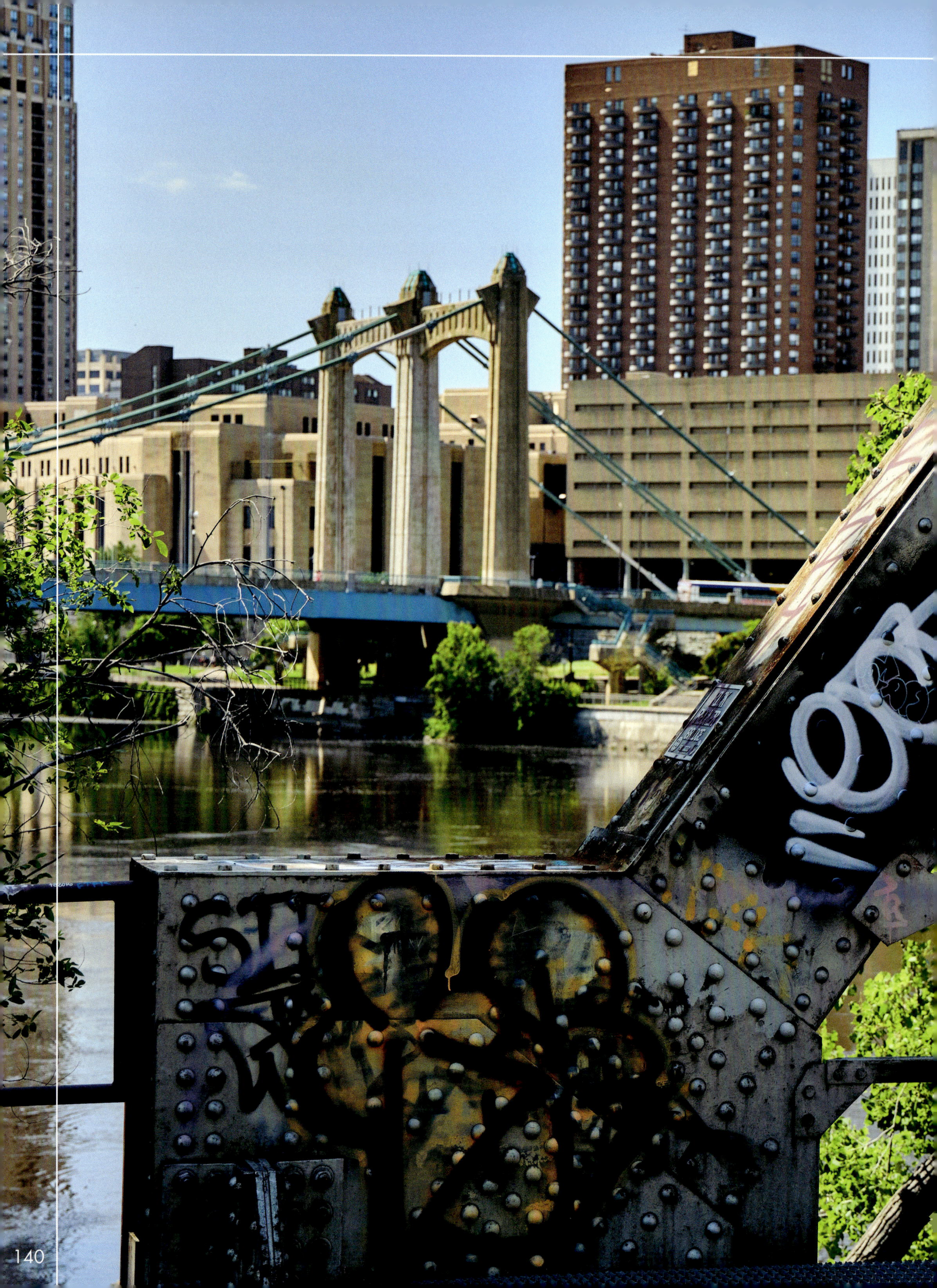

Bios

Reverend Shawn Morrison

Ministering hope, one act of kindness at a time

Reverend Shawn Morrison is a seasoned minister, nonprofit leader, and community advocate with over 30 years of experience. He is the Founder and Executive Director of Good in the 'Hood, a Twin Cities-based nonprofit dedicated to inspiring intentional kindness and community outreach. His leadership background includes pastoral ministry, higher education, and urban outreach, with previous roles at Cedarcrest Free Methodist Church, Bethany Global University, and Union Gospel Mission Twin Cities. He also brings valuable experience as a chaplain supporting individuals facing mental health and addiction challenges. Shawn and his wife, Jamie, have five children and nineteen grandchildren.

Shawn Nielsen

Commercial photographer with a heart

Shawn Nielsen is a 36-year veteran commercial photographer with a passion for people. Shawn has a heart for creating images that reveal the beauty, strength and fragility of the human spirit. He founded Nielsen Studios, in Rogers, Minnesota, in 2003. In his personal life, as in the images he creates, Shawn strives always to make a positive impact in the lives of others. Shawn and his wife, Cristine, have four children and two grandchildren.

142

Endorsements

Thank you, Pastor Shawn Morrison and Mr. Shawn Nielsen, for introducing us to those who often go unnoticed. Jesus teaches us to love our neighbor as ourselves; but how can we truly love if we do not take the time to know?   — *Danielle Igbanugo, Founder of 3000 Acts Of Kindness by Coated In Love*

After learning about the material in this book, I've become a friend to those experiencing homelessness. I have begun to keep things in my car that might be helpful including socks, bottles of water, and food. I'm always watching so I can stop, pay attention and be a friend.   — *Reverend Vernon Eng*

"Will You See Me?" has totally changed how I think about and engage with people in need. I used to think that if I didn't have money to give or something to offer that I should ignore and look away. Now, I smile, wave and say hello. This project has given me, my wife and our daughters a new perspective on what it means to be human.   — *Reverend Neil Essen*

The perspective in the book "Will You See Me?" has made a real difference in the way I perceive and engage with people that I encounter who are in need. In the past I wasn't sure if I had anything to offer them. In fact, I was concerned that my engagement might create harm. I now see people in need with new eyes. I see them as people who have the same needs for love and acceptance that I do. I have learned to apply the platinum rule: "Do unto others as you would have them do unto you."   — *Robb Breding, CEO REV Advisory Group*